C000220546

George Baker

A COOK FOR ALL SEASONS

Boxtree

First published in Great Britain in 1989 by Boxtree Limited

Designed by Peter Ward

Illustrations by Amy Roberts

Edited by Susie Ward

Typeset by
Cambrian Typesetters, Frimley, Surrey

Printed in Great Britain by
Richard Clay Ltd, Bungay, Suffolk

for Boxtree Limited
36 Tavistock Street
London
WC2E 7PB

BRITISH LIBRARY CATALOGUING IN PUBLICATION DATA
Baker, George
A cook for all seasons.
1. Food, Recipes
I. Title
641.5

ISBN 1-85283-254-1

CONTENTS

INTRODUCTION

I DO like to see pleasure on the faces of my friends when they eat with us. This is not very far removed from what I feel about acting. Thinking about the play, the preparation of my part and, finally, the presentation to the audience is much the same as thinking about the menu, the preparation and, finally, the presentation of the dinner.

Just before the curtain rises or the front door bell rings there is a delicious moment of anticipation and a frightening moment of self doubt; very soon you will know if your expectations are to be rewarded. The audience listens, laughs and appreciates; your guests eat, enjoy and smile. At least that's how it always is in my dreams.

Cooking is an integral part of my life; I would get withdrawal symptoms if I was abruptly cut off from a kitchen. At about the age of seven I knew that I wanted to be an actor – at about the same age I started to haunt the kitchen. Stealing prunes, licking out mixing bowls, cutting my fingers were the sort of activities that made me feel thoroughly at home there. I still keep a bag of nuts or prunes handy in the corner of some cupboard, just in case I need to sort out a problem or I'm supposed to be on a diet.

I have cooked in bed-sits, over camp fires, in a hotel kitchen and at home. The beef olives bought in Glasgow and cooked over a fire of driftwood on the beach at Wemyss Bay, one sunlit September day, remain in the memory. I was touring with the Old Vic at the time, playing John Worthing in *The Importance of Being Earnest*, doubling the Porter and one of the witches in *Macbeth*, and playing the Earl of Warwick in *St Joan*. We toured England for 13 weeks and then went to Moscow, Leningrad and Warsaw. I collected a great many recipes then and have continued to do so. I have recipes from America, France, the Middle East, Bulgaria, Australia, Ireland and many other countries, and delight in mixing menus from different parts of the world.

In writing this book I hope to convey some of the pleasure I have had as a cook, and itinerant actor.

George Baker.

Winter

I WAS born in Varna, Bulgaria, of an Irish mother and a Yorkshire father, in April 1931. My mother tells me that it was a cold morning – so cold that the doctor kept piling wood into the green, tiled stove in the corner of the room. The fire became so hot that it set fire to the chimney. The Fire Brigade was called.

My brother and my father both had whooping cough and were in bed in their respective bedrooms. A screen was put around my mother and she gave birth to me as the firemen trooped in and out of the bedroom. The date was April 1st, so it was really quite inevitable that I would one day want to be an actor.

For the first nine years of my life I ate yoghurt, kebabs, stuffed peppers and vine leaves, meat on skewers and all sorts of beans and salads. Soups were important too – yoghurt and walnut, bortsch, and cold cucumber among them. Apricots, walnuts, figs, cherries, melons and tomatoes were there for the picking. Hot bread rings sprinkled with sesame seed were sold in the street. We grew our own grapes and made our own wine. When the H.M.S. *London* docked at Varna in 1938, my mother and father entertained the officers and ship's complement at the villa. I helped to carry the wine jugs from the barrels to the tables. I was later found beside one of the barrels, tipsy and fast asleep.

Those long-gone summers were hot and the winters properly cold. And the tastes acquired in childhood have stayed with me all my life.

MENU 1

IMAM BAYALDU

FILLET OF PORK

STEAMED CABBAGE AND CARAWAY

SAUTÉED PEPPERS

BAKED APPLES IN VANILLA SYRUP

Imam Bayaldu

SERVES 6

CLAUDIA RODEN in her book *Middle Eastern Food* gives Iman Bayaldi as a Turkish speciality, but the Bulgarians claim it as theirs. After 500 years of domination it would be difficult to know if the Turkish armies brought the dish with them or found it and took it home. Miss Roden gives the story that the Turkish priest fainted when he was served these stuffed aubergines by his wife. Whatever the origin it is a delightful starter.

WORKING TIME: 1 hour standing time. 30 minutes preparation time. 1 hour cooking time.

3 medium aubergines
Salt and freshly ground black pepper
3 tomatoes
2 onions, peeled
2 cloves garlic finely chopped
2 carrots
1 stalk celery
Juice of ½ lemon
1 tablespoon chopped parsley
1 teaspoon paprika
2 tablespoons breadcrumbs
150 ml/5 fl oz sunflower oil

Remove the stalk from the aubergines and cut them in half. Cut out the seedy centre of each aubergine, salt the thick shell and leave it to stand for an hour. Wash away the bitter juices and dry the aubergines.

Scald the tomatoes and remove the skin. Chop roughly. Finely chop the onions, put into a frying pan and pour over a little oil to soften. Add the garlic to the oil.

Take the vegetables off the heat and stir in the tomatoes, chopped parsley and the lemon juice. Season to taste with salt and pepper and the paprika. Stuff the aubergines with the mixture and sprinkle the breadcrumbs over them.

Put the stuffed aubergines into a baking dish, pour the sunflower oil and 2 tablespoons water over them and cover with greaseproof paper. Cook in a 180°C/350°F/Gas mark 4 oven for an hour, or until soft.

Leave them to cool and serve cold.

Fillet of Pork

SERVES 6

WORKING TIME: 20 minutes preparation time. Approximately 10 minutes cooking time.

2 large pork fillets
1 tablespoon tomato purée
Paprika
225 g/8 oz flat chopped mushrooms
2 cloves garlic, crushed
200 g/7 oz fetta cheese, crumbled
1 tablespoon finely chopped parsley
1 tablespoon lemon juice
50 g/2 oz butter
Salt

Trim and skin the pork fillet. Cut them into oblong pieces and flatten them between two sheets of greaseproof paper with the palm of your hand. Spread the fillets with tomato purée and sprinkle with paprika to taste. Set aside.

Put the mushrooms, garlic, cheese and parsley into a saucepan with the butter and the lemon juice and cook until the mushrooms are soft and the whole can be blended into a paste. Season the stuffing with salt to taste.

Put a little stuffing on each fillet, roll it up, and tie with string. Grill under a medium high flame for 10 minutes or until the rolls are browned and cooked through.

Steamed Cabbage and Caraway

SERVES 6

WORKING TIME: 5 minutes preparation time. 5 minutes cooking time.

1 medium Savoy cabbage
1 teaspoon caraway seeds
2 tablespoons butter
Salt and freshly ground black pepper

very thinly, put it into a steamer and put the steamer over the saucepan. Add the caraway seeds.

Steam the cabbage for about 5 minutes, then transfer the cabbage to a warm serving dish and add the butter, and salt and pepper to taste.

Sautéed Peppers

SERVES 6

WORKING TIME: 30–40 minutes preparation and cooking time.

2 green sweet peppers
2 red sweet peppers
4 shallots, peeled and sliced
50 g/2 oz butter
1 tablespoon lemon juice
1 tablespoon finely chopped dill

Cut the tops off the peppers, take out the seeds and cut away the ribs. Cut the peppers into squares of about 2.5 cm (1 in).

Pour 150 ml (¼ pint) water into a frying pan and bring it to the boil. Put the shallots in and cook for 5 minutes or so, until the water has almost evaporated and the shallots are tender. Add the butter, lemon juice and peppers and cook for another 5 minutes or until the vegetables are tender. You will need to stir all the time. At the last minute sprinkle on the chopped dill.

Baked Apples in Vanilla Syrup

SERVES 6

WORKING TIME: 30 minutes preparation time. 15 minutes cooking time.

6 medium-sized cooking apples
75 g/3 oz of walnut kernels
50 g/2 oz butter
150 g/5 oz sugar
300 ml/½ pt Vanilla Syrup
(see page 142)
½ teaspoon cinnamon

Peel the apples, remove the cores and set aside. Crush the walnuts. Reserve.

Beat the butter in a small bowl. Mix in the sugar, cinnamon and crushed walnuts. Stuff the apples with this mixture and arrange the apples in a baking dish. Pour 2 tablespoons water over them and bake in a 180°C/350°F/Gas mark 4 oven for about 45 minutes, or until soft and pulpy.

The baked apples can be served hot or cold. If you are serving them cold, pour the Vanilla Syrup over them and allow them to cool together.

THERE was a storm over the Black Sea in October 1938. I remember it well because it blew a great many quail off their migratory course. Some fell exhausted and dying into the garden of our house in Varna.

My father was a Yorkshireman who had settled in Bulgaria after the end of the First World War. He was a farmer's son from Wetherby who had decided to join his uncle's export/import firm in Moscow. When war broke out in 1914, he returned from Russia to join the Royal Warwickshire Regiment. After serving with them in France he was posted to the Balkan Front at the end of 1916.

He liked Bulgaria and set up his business there after the war. He was a good shot and we often had game which he brought home to be cleaned and cooked.

However, seeing the small, exhausted quail in our garden was different. They lay fluttering on the ground in one corner where two walls provided some shelter. Father went out to look at them. My brother and I watched him. Some of the quail he killed; others he picked up and put into an outhouse. We gave them corn; two days later most of them had flown on their way.

Wild quail have decreased enormously in number and they are now farmed to supply the tables of the West.

MENU 2

BRIOCHE OF SALMON PÂTÉ

JUGGED HARE

PURÉE OF ROOT VEGETABLES

MASHED POTATOES

LEMON CREAM

Brioche of Salmon Pâté

SERVES 6

WORKING TIME: 2 hours preparation time. 2 hours standing time. 30 minutes cooking time.

FOR THE BRIOCHE

2 tablespoons barely tepid milk
2 teaspoons baker's yeast
150 g/5 oz of plain flour
1 teaspoon salt
1 teaspoon sugar
2 eggs
125 g/4½ oz of butter

FOR THE PÂTÉ

225 g/8 oz of fresh salmon steak
1 small tin anchovies
50 g/2 oz smoked salmon pieces
1 tablespoon lemon juice
1 egg white
150 ml/5 fl oz white wine
¼ teaspoon fenugreek powder
150 ml/5 fl oz cream

Heat the milk, but very gently. It should be barely tepid. Mix into it the 2 teaspoons of baker's yeast.

Put the flour into a bowl and scoop out a well in the centre. Add the salt and the sugar. Break 2 eggs into the well; add the yeast and milk mixture. Knead the mixture until the dough is smooth. Soften the butter and add this to the dough. Roll it into a ball.

Sprinkle a wooden bowl with flour. Put the dough ball into it and cut a cross in the dough with a knife. Cover with a light cloth and put it in an airing cupboard or a similarly warm place. In 2 hours it should have risen to twice its original size.

Take the dough out of the bowl and knead it lightly again. Then cover it with a light cloth and put it to stand in a cool place until you require it.

Bring the white wine and the lemon juice to the boil in a saucepan. Poach the salmon in it for 5 minutes. Allow the fish to cool. Remove the skin and any bones it may have. Flake it roughly.

Put the flaked fish in the blender with the tin of anchovies, their oil, and the smoked salmon pieces. Add the cream and the fenugreek powder. Blend them all together.

Whip the white of egg and fold it into the salmon pâté. Scrape the pâté into a bowl. Put some water into a baking dish. Stand the bowl of pâté in it and heat through very gently in the oven.

Lightly rub a baking tin with butter. Spread the brioche dough on the tin and flatten into an oblong shape with your hand. Sprinkle flour on it and turn it over.

Take the warm pâté from its bowl and place it in the centre of the brioche dough. Wet your fingers with cold water, gather up the corners of the brioche dough and wrap the pâté in it, pinching the edges and the top.

Let the stuffed brioche stand for 15 minutes, then cook in a 180°C/350°F/ Gas mark 4 oven for 30 minutes.

Jugged Hare

SERVES 6

WORKING TIME: 30 minutes preparation time. 2 hours cooking time. (This dish can be made the day before and reheated.)

1 medium-sized hare
Freshly ground black pepper
2 tablespoons oatmeal
50 g/2 oz beef dripping
5 shallots
10 cloves
1 lemon
1 apple (2 crab apples if you can get them)
7 or 8 mushrooms
900 ml/1½ pt Brown Stock (see page 126)
1 glass claret
1 sachet bouquet garni

FOR THE FORCEMEAT BALLS (OPTIONAL)

2 slices lean bacon
150 g/5 oz breadcrumbs
2 eggs
2 tablespoons oil
1 tablespoon mixed fresh herbs – parsley, thyme, mint, nutmeg
Rind of ½ lemon

Ask your butcher to skin, draw and joint the hare for you and reserve the blood. You will need a good heavy earthenware jug, or pot. The head should be cooked in this dish if you are doing it traditionally, but some are squeamish.

Pepper the joints and flour them lightly with oatmeal. Fry them in the dripping until they are lightly browned.

Put the rib joints, the liver and the blood of the hare at the bottom of a large pot or casserole. (If you do use the head you should put that at the bottom too.) Sprinkle a little oatmeal over the first layer. Peel the shallots and stick them full of cloves. Add them to the pot and then top with more hare. Slice the apple and lemon and add them to the casserole. Sprinkle with more pepper and oatmeal. Add the mushrooms and the glass of claret. Put in the sachet of bouquet garni with the string hanging out so that you can remove it when the time comes. Pour Brown Stock over the layers to cover.

Seal the casserole tightly by putting a piece of greaseproof paper over it before putting on the lid. Stand the pot in a large saucepan of water and cook in a preheated 180°C/350°F/Gas mark 4 oven. This will take about 3 hours.

You can garnish this dish with forcemeat balls, if desired. To make, beat the eggs and mix all the other ingredients together. Use the eggs to bind the mixture. Divide into balls and fry golden-brown.

You can either serve the hare from the 'jug' or heat a large serving dish and arrange the meat attractively on it, surrounded by the forcemeat balls.

Redcurrant jelly goes well with jugged hare.

Purée of Root Vegetables

SERVES 6

WORKING TIME: 10 minutes preparation time. 15 minutes cooking time.

2 parsnips
2 turnips
4 carrots
1 tablespoon sunflower oil
2 tablespoons butter
Salt and freshly ground black pepper

Peel, wash and dice the vegetables. Cook them in the oil – as little oil as it takes to cover the bottom of your pan.

When soft put them through a blender or food processor; add the butter, salt to taste and plenty of black pepper.

Mashed Potatoes

SERVES 6

WORKING TIME: 10 minutes preparation time. 20 minutes cooking time.

8 medium potatoes
1 egg
2 tablespoons butter
150 ml/¼ pt milk
Salt and freshly ground black pepper

Bring 600 ml (1 pt) water to the boil in a saucepan. Wash the potatoes, but don't peel them. Put them into the boiling water and cook. Test with a fork and when they are tender remove them from the water. Let them stand for a moment and then peel them. Pour the potato water into a bowl and keep for soup.

Put the potatoes back into the saucepan and cover with a cloth. Heat over a medium heat for 2 to 3 minutes. They will now be good and flaky. Mash them with a fork and add the butter, egg and the milk. Salt and pepper to taste.

(To make soup later, cook a potato or so more than you need. Soften some leeks or an onion in butter and a little of the potato water. Put your spare potatoes and your leek or onion through a blender or food processor, adding some fresh basil, a pinch of fenugreek, salt, pepper and a tablespoon or two of cream. The result is a delightful soup.)

Lemon Cream

SERVES 6

THIS is a recipe my great-grandmother left in one of her recipe books. Though I know my grandmother died in 1911, I don't know when my great-grandmother died – possibly in the 1870s. So it's an old Yorkshire recipe. In another recipe she talks of 'taking a pound of Keswick apples'. I wish that so many varieties of English apples had not been lost with time and 'progress'.

WORKING TIME: 15 minutes preparation time. (This is best made the day before.)

1½ lemons
175 g/6 oz caster sugar
3 glasses sweet sherry
450 ml/¾ pt double cream

Grate one lemon and put the rind into a mixing bowl. Squeeze the lemon and the half lemon and add the juice to the bowl. Mix in the sugar.

Add the sherry and stir it until the sugar dissolves. Pour in the cream; whisk until the mixture is quite thick. Pour it into glasses.

Allow the glasses to stand in a cool place or refrigerator for 1 day. At the end of this time the liquid at the bottom of the glass should be clear and the cream quite firm on top.

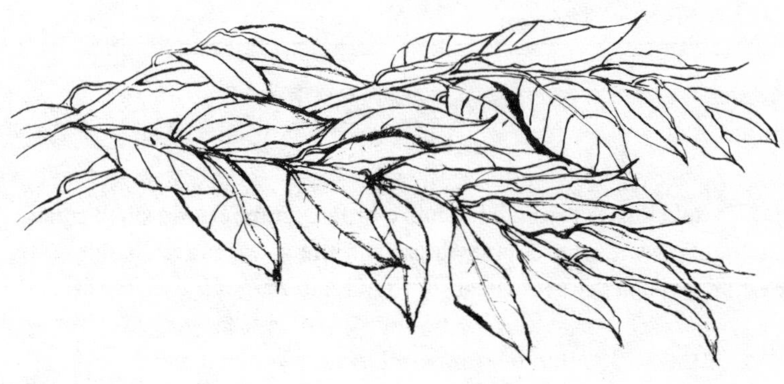

We came home from Bulgaria in 1940, leaving my father behind to come out with the British Legation and go to Cairo. He died there in 1942.

We took the last Simplon Express out of Sofia. It should have been a comfortable journey to Paris, but the train was stopped by the Italians in Milan. We were kept there for three days and it seemed probable that we might be interned. However, mother used her charm, her diplomatic status and her Irishness. She was known in the hotel as 'Signora Irlandese con cinque bambini'.

We continued our journey very uncomfortably. The Cook's Tour guide leaned in at the window as the train was leaving Milan station and stole our passports and our money. When we reached Paris, we found the British Embassy there crowded with refugees but helpful and generous. Mother took us around the city not knowing if we would ever see it again, or what the war would bring.

She took the two eldest to the Bal Tabarin, basically a very classy strip club, on the assumption that it might not be there when we grew up. We were treated with great curiosity as I was only nine and my brother barely twelve. Paris fell to the Germans four weeks later, ten days after we left for England.

MENU 3

GREEN PEA SOUP

BEEF OLIVES

CARROTS AND CARAWAY

ENGLISH SPINACH

FLAMBÉED PEACHES IN CALVADOS

Green Pea Soup

SERVES 6

THIS soup is delicious served cold. Chop a little cucumber into small squares and use them, together with more mint, to garnish the soup. For a change of flavour, use soured cream or yoghurt instead of the cream or milk.

WORKING TIME: 35 minutes preparation and cooking time.

1 good-sized Spanish onion
1 tablespoon butter
900 ml/1½ pt Ham Bone stock (see page 126)
450 g/1 lb bag of frozen peas, thawed
2 teaspoons chopped parsley
1 teaspoon chopped chervil
2 teaspoons chopped mint
600 ml/1 pt Vegetable Stock (see page 128) or water
2 teaspoons lemon juice
1 tablespoon milk or cream

Peel and slice the onion. Fry in a pan with the butter and a tablespoon of Ham Bone Stock until soft. Add the peas and the rest of the ham stock and bring to the boil. Simmer gently for 4 minutes then add the herbs and simmer for 2 minutes more. Pour the soup into a blender or food processor and blend it until it is smooth. Put it through a sieve and then back into the pan. Add as much of the Vegetable Stock or water as will bring it to a thick liquid consistency. Flavour with the lemon juice and salt and pepper to taste. Finally, stir in the cream or milk. Reheat the soup gently, taking care not to boil. Serve immediately.

Beef Olives

SERVES 6

WORKING TIME: 35 minutes preparation time. 1 hour cooking time.

575 g/1¼ lb rump steak
4 fresh or tinned anchovy fillets
1 tablespoon chopped parsley
1 teaspoon butter
75 g/3 oz breadcrumbs
2 teaspoons lemon juice
1 egg
Salt and freshly ground black pepper
2 shallots
1 tablespoon oil
1 tablespoon flour
600 ml/1 pt Brown Stock (see page 126)
1 glass claret

Ask your butcher to cut the rump steak into thin slices. Ask him to beat it for you like veal escalopes. When you return home, cut the steak into strips 7.5 cm × 4 cm (3 in × 1½ in) wide. Put them to one side while you make the forcemeat.

Put the anchovies, butter, parsley, breadcrumbs and lemon juice into a blender or food processor and blend. Scrape into a bowl and mix in the egg. Add salt and pepper to taste. Spoon a little of the forcemeat onto a strip of beef, roll it up and tie with a string. Repeat with the remaining strips.

Peel and chop the shallots. Put them in a pan with the oil, add the beef olives and fry, turning them over to brown them. Remove from the pan and drain.

Put the flour in with the shallots. Add the stock and wine gradually to make a smooth brown gravy. Return the beef olives to the pan and simmer gently for 1 hour. Just before serving remove the string from the beef olives.

Carrots and Caraway

SERVES 6

WORKING TIME: 5 minutes preparation time. 15 minutes working time.

8 or 10 medium carrots
2 tablespoons butter
1 teaspoon caraway seeds
Salt

Cut the carrots into halves or quarters. Put them into boiling water and cook till tender. Drain them and dry on a cloth. Return the carrots to the saucepan with the butter and caraway seeds. Salt to taste.

English Spinach

SERVES 6

WORKING TIME: 5 minutes preparation time. 5 minutes cooking time.

900 g/2 lb winter spinach with good big leaves
Butter
Salt and freshly ground black pepper

Thoroughly wash and dry the spinach. Bring 150 ml/5 fl oz water to the boil in a wide saucepan. Lay the leaves of the spinach flat in the saucepan. Cover and let them cook through. Drain off all the water and dry the leaves in a cloth. Put the spinach back into the saucepan and toss in the butter. Salt and pepper to taste.

Flambéed Peaches in Calvados

SERVES 6

WORKING TIME: 7 minutes cooking time.

2 × 400 g/14 oz tins peaches
8 tablespoons Calvados

Put the peaches and their syrup in a saucepan with 6 tablespoons of the Calvados. Let this heat through slowly. Heat a serving dish. At the last minute heat the rest of the Calvados in another saucepan. Arrange the peaches on the hot serving dish. Pour on the hot Calvados and light with a match. Serve immediately.

WE arrived in Dublin in June 1940. Aunt Avis, my uncle's wife, taught me elocution and we won the junior medal at the Father Matthew Fois. I recited a piece by W. B. Yeats, a poet I still love. After my experience of the Fois I was quite determined to be an actor.

I couldn't eat enough barm brack and learnt to bake soda bread, a wonderful bread and easy to make. It goes wonderfully well with pâté or soup.

As for the luscious dish of shallots, remember that garlic and onions need not smell if they are properly cooked.

> 'There is in every cook's opinion,
> No savoury dish without an onion;
> But lest your kissing should be spoiled
> The onion must be thoroughly boiled.'

So said JONATHAN SWIFT (1667–1745).

MENU 4

LEEK AND POTATO SOUP
SODA BREAD

OX TONGUE PIQUANTE
GLAZED SHALLOTS
PARSNIP AND CARROT PURÉE

HONEY MOUSSE

Leek and Potato Soup

SERVES 6

WORKING TIME: 15 minutes preparation time. 40 minutes cooking time.

575 g/1¼ lb potatoes
4 medium-sized leeks
1 onion
4 tablespoons butter or oil
2 teaspoons lemon juice
1.4–1.75 litres/2½–3 pt White or Vegetable Stock (see pages 127 and 128)
Salt and freshly ground black pepper
150 ml/5 fl oz double cream

Peel and slice the potatoes. Peel and slice the onion and leeks.

Put the butter and the lemon juice in a saucepan and heat until the butter is melted. Add the sliced potatoes, the leeks and the lemons. Cook until tender but do not allow to overcook and brown.

Slowly add the stock, the salt and the pepper. Allow to simmer gently for 30 to 35 minutes. Add more water, if necessary. Put in a food processor or blender and mix. Pour the puréed soup back into the pan, reheat but take care not to boil. Mix in the cream.

Soda Bread

MAKES LOAF

WORKING TIME: 15 minutes preparation time. 35 minutes cooking time.

350 g/12 oz brown flour
175 g/6 oz white flour
1 teaspoon cream of tartar
1 teaspoon bicarbonate of soda
Salt
150 ml/5 fl oz soured milk
1 teaspoon lemon juice

Mix the brown and white flours in a bowl. Mix the cream of tartar and the bicarbonate of soda into a sieve and sprinkle onto the flour. Add a pinch of salt.

Make a well in the flour. If you can't get hold of soured milk you can sour your own by putting a teaspoonful of lemon into the milk. Put the soured milk into the well of the flour and mix lightly; don't knead the bread. Mix as quickly as you can then pat the dough into a round.

Put the round on a floured baking sheet and cut a cross in the top. I always let it stand for a moment near some heat before putting it in the oven.

Preheat the oven to 180°C/350°F/Gas mark 4 and bake for 35 minutes. You can tell when the bread is done by pushing a skewer into its centre. It should come out clean. Leave the loaf to cool on a cooling rack for at least 4 hours.

Ox Tongue Piquante

SERVES 6

THE piquante sauce for the ox tongue is from a recipe by Michael Kelly, an Irish composer who became director of music at The Theatre Royal, Drury Lane. Later he enjoyed a great success in Italy, way back in 1822.

WORKING TIME: 30 minutes cooking time.

12 slices of ox tongue
2 tablespoons oil
1 small glass dry sherry, brandy or Calvados
3 hard-boiled egg yolks
1 tin filleted anchovies
1 tablespoon capers
1 tablespoon vinegar
1 tablespoon English mustard powder
1 tablespoon parsley
1 shallot, chopped
Salt and freshly ground black pepper
150 g/5 oz Brown Gravy (see page 139)

Put the slices of ox tongue in a braising dish with a tablespoon of oil and a glass of your chosen wine. Let it heat through very slowly. Do not allow it to boil.

Put all the other ingredients except the Brown Gravy into a food processor and blend until smooth.

Put the gravy in a saucepan and heat. Add the blended mixture to the gravy. Stir until thoroughly heated through. Serve with the ox tongue.

Glazed Shallots

SERVES 6

WORKING TIME: 15 minutes preparation time. 25 minutes cooking time.

800 g/1¾ lb shallots
3 tablespoons butter
1 tablespoon soft brown sugar
175 ml/6 fl oz Vegetable Stock (see page 128)
1 tablespoon lemon juice
1 tablespoon freshly chopped dill

Peel the shallots. Melt the butter in a big frying pan. Put the shallots in the pan – they can rub shoulders in it but no more overcrowding than that. Sprinkle over the sugar. Add the stock and the lemon juice.

Shake the pan from time to time to turn the shallots. Cook until most of the liquid has evaporated. Sprinkle over the chopped dill and serve.

Parsnip and Carrot Purée

SERVES 6

WORKING TIME: 10 minutes preparation time. 30 minutes cooking time.

450 g/1 lb parsnips
450 g/1 lb carrots
4 tablespoons butter
Salt and freshly ground black pepper
150 ml/¼ pt Vegetable Stock (see page 128) or water
1 teaspoon lemon juice
1 tablespoon cream

Peel, wash and slice the parsnips and the carrots. Melt half the butter and two spoonfuls of the stock or water in a good heavy saucepan. Put in the carrots and the parsnips and allow to cook slowly until they are soft. It may be that you will have to add a little more stock or water, but keep this at a minimum as it is best to sweat the vegetables.

Put the vegetables and any liquid into a blender or food processor and purée. Put them back in the pan and heat adding the remaining butter and the cream. Salt to taste and add a good grinding of black pepper. Serve straight away.

Honey Mousse

SERVES 6

WORKING TIME: (This mousse should be made the day before, or several hours before use.) 10 minutes preparation time. 30 minutes cooking time.

3 eggs
300 ml/½ pt runny honey (Greek honey is very good)

Separate the eggs and whisk the whites. Put them in the fridge to chill.

Put the honey and the eggs into a double boiler and cook very slowly over a low heat stirring all the time until the mixture thickens and becomes custard-like.

Take it off the heat and let it cool.

Take the whites out of the fridge and whisk again. When the custard mixture has cooled fold in the whites. Spoon into individual glasses and refrigerate for several hours before serving.

IT was back to England in 1941, mother feeling that, as English children, we should spend the war in England.

We were all put to board in various schools while mother went to London to work as a monitor in the Bulgarian section of the B.B.C. We spent some holidays in a holiday home in Green Hammerton, just outside York.

It was the first time I had met an Aga. Winnie Harborough was the splendid Scotswoman who cooked for the home. She taught me the rudiments of discipline in the kitchen and allowed me to rake and fill the Aga night and morning. Her husband, Ernest, a lieutenant in the Navy, took me to see Greenwich when he was convalescing, after being wounded in action. Many years later I bumped into them in Princes Street, Edinburgh, while on tour with the Old Vic. I invited them to a performance of St Joan.

In 1942 my father died in Cairo. My mother became ill and left her job with the B.B.C. She rented a cottage in Sussex and there she tried to make a home for us. Money was very tight – in fact, almost non-existent. I became quite a hand at pastry and we ate a great many vegetable pies. The local gamekeeper kept us supplied with rabbits, a hare or two and sometimes a pheasant. He taught me how to skin, or pluck and draw.

Mother taught me a great deal about cooking; when she was interested she was a very good cook. At this time we were cooking on a four-burner Valor Perfection oil stove; when you wanted to roast you put the oven, which was separate, over two of the rings.

My bible was a cook-book I found called *Warne's Everyday Cookery*. It must have been published in the Twenties but the kitchen maxims bear repeating:

A place for everything and everything in its place.
Clear as you go and so avoid muddle.
Endeavour to make the most of everything.
Save the bones of meat and the carcasses of poultry for stock.
Never leave soups, stocks or sauces standing in a pan all night.
Save gravy or sauces that are left over; they are useful in various made-up dishes.
Save all scraps of fat; they can be clarified.
Plan a whole day's meals at a time.
Read all recipes through carefully and have all ingredients ready before beginning to make any dish.
Remember to please the eye as well as the palate.

MENU 5

MUSHROOMS STUFFED WITH CRAB

SPICED HAM AND BRANDIED PEACHES

CELERIAC GRATIN

APPLE SNOW

Mushrooms Stuffed with Crab

SERVES 6

WORKING TIME: 25 minutes preparation time. 10 minutes cooking time.

24 large firm mushrooms
1 large Spanish onion
4 cloves garlic
100 g/4 oz butter
1 tablespoon sunflower oil
Salt and freshly ground black pepper
800 g/1¾ lb crab meat
1 tablespoon chopped fresh or dried basil
100 g/4 oz dried breadcrumbs or lightly fried and crumbled croutons
1 tablespoon Dijon mustard
200 g/7 oz grated Cheddar or Gruyère cheese

Peel and stem the mushrooms. Finely chop the mushroom stems, the onion and the garlic by hand or use a food processor or blender. Put this in a sauté pan with the crab meat and cook in the butter and oil. Add the basil, salt and pepper to taste. Now stir in the breadcrumbs and the mustard.

Spoon a little of the filling into each mushroom cap. Sprinkle over the grated cheese. Bake in a 190°C/375°F/Gas mark 5 oven for about 10 minutes. Serve warm.

Spiced Ham and Brandied Peaches

SERVES 8 OR MORE

WORKING TIME: 12 hours soaking time. Between 3–5½ hours cooking time.

4–6 kg/9–13 lb cured ham
300 ml/½ pt cider
1 lemon
1 teaspoon nutmeg
2 tablespoons Demerara sugar
1 tablespoon breadcrumbs
1 teaspoon ground cloves
2 tablespoons honey
1 glass dry sherry
2 × 900 g/2 lb tin peach halves
175 g/6 oz caster sugar
150 ml/¼ pt of brandy
Almond essence

Wash the ham well, cover with water and let it soak for 12 hours.

Put it in a pan with the cider and water to cover.

Cut the lemon in half and put that into the water with the ham. Add the nutmeg and bring to the boil. Then turn down the heat and simmer for 20–25 minutes per 450 g/1 lb.

When the ham is ready, cut away the skin. It should come away very easily.

In a bowl blend together the sugar, breadcrumbs and cloves. Spread the mixure over the ham. Cook in a 190°C/375°F/Gas mark 5 oven for 15 minutes. The sugar must be melted.

Now pour the honey and dry sherry over the ham and return to the oven for another 15 minutes.

To make the brandied peaches, drain the peaches but keep 300 ml (½ pt) of the juice to one side. Mix the sugar and the peach juice and reduce over the heat to half the quantity. Cool and stir in the brandy and the almond essence to taste.

Pour the brandy syrup over the peaches and serve with the ham.

Celeriac Gratin

SERVES 8

WORKING TIME: 25 minutes preparation time. 15 minutes cooking time.

2 large roots celeriac
1 tablespoon sunflower oil
2 shallots
2 tablespoons butter
150 ml/¼ pt Vegetable or White Stock (see pages 128 and 127)
2 tablespoons flour
4 tablespoons grated Cheddar cheese
150 ml/5 fl oz milk
Salt
Paprika
1 tablespoon chopped parsley

Peel the celeriac and cut it into medium slices. Put the oil and 1 tablespoon water in a saucepan, add the celeriac and cook until it is tender.

Chop the shallots. Soften them in the butter and a little stock in another saucepan. Add the flour and stir in well. Now add half the cheese, the remaining stock and the milk. Season with salt and paprika to taste.

Put the celeriac in a fireproof dish and pour over the sauce. Sprinkle over the rest of the cheese.

Preheat the grill to medium high. Put the celeriac under the grill until it is golden-brown. Sprinkle it with the parsley and serve.

Apple Snow

SERVES 6

WORKING TIME: 25 minutes preparation and cooking time.

3 large cooking apples
Rind of ½ lemon
2 cloves
100 g/4 oz caster sugar
3 egg whites

Wash, peel and core the apples. Slice them and put them into a pan with the lemon – rind, cloves and all – and 3 tablespoons water. Simmer until the apples are tender.

Remove them from the heat, take out the cloves and the lemon, and stir in the sugar. Put them into a food processor or blender and reduce to a purée.

Whip the egg whites until they are stiff and fold into the apple purée. Pour into a soufflé dish and chill until ready to serve.

ON a grey morning in 1943 I was given the responsibility of seeing that my sister, two of my brothers and I, got from York to Wisborough Green in Sussex, to join our mother for the school holidays. We caught the Flying Scot, the 10:10 from York.

I was twelve years old, my sister was eight, one brother was seven, the other three-and-a-half. Our older brother was travelling by the same train, but he had found a seat with friends. Some soldiers found room for us on their kitbags in the corridor.

Five hours later the train pulled into King's Cross. I had been told to take the underground from King's Cross to London Bridge. From London Bridge we were to go to Billingshurst, where a taxi would be waiting to take us home – a cottage mother had rented about two miles outside Wisborough Green.

I was carrying my youngest brother and the other two were each holding a corner of my mac. As we got onto the train the doors closed, leaving my younger brother on the platform.

We got out at the next station, The Angel, hoping to see him on the train and catch up with him. He didn't seem to be on it so we returned to King's Cross. No seven-year-old had handed himself over to the station-master for safe-keeping. I was advised to go to London Bridge and see the station-master there. I had just got to the office to report the missing brother when he was brought in by a porter. He had been caught trying to slip through the ticket barrier without a ticket. He told the porter that his big brother was lost but that he was on his way home to Billingshurst. We were reunited and very relieved. The train we should have caught had left with our older brother on it. We took the next train.

The taxi from Billingshurst had left with our older brother in it. We took a bus that went from Billingshurst to Petworth. Our nearest stop left us about a mile to walk through the woods. My mother met us in the hall. 'Ah, there you are, George', she said. 'Feed the children! I'm writing a novel.' It was an invitation I couldn't refuse.

We had omelettes made with dried eggs that night and I put the oats on to soak for porridge the next morning. There's no better way of learning to cook than having to do it.

MENU 6

CREAM OF CELERIAC SOUP WITH DICED ANCHOVIES

CHICKEN WITH GRAPES

HARICOT BEANS WITH ALMONDS

SAUTÉED SPINACH AND FENNEL

CHERRY FRASCATI

Cream of Celeriac Soup with Diced Anchovies

SERVES 6

WORKING TIME: 15 minutes preparation time. 30 minutes cooking time.

450 g/1 lb celeriac
1 tablespoon oil
1.4 litres/2½ pt Vegetable Stock (see page 128)
150 ml/¼ pt double cream
1 small tin anchovy fillets
1 tablespoon finely chopped celery tops
Salt and freshly ground black pepper

Wash and peel the celeriac. Cut it into thin slices.

Mix the oil and 1 tablespoon of water in a saucepan. Put in the celeriac, cover the saucepan and cook over a slow heat until soft. (You might have to add a little water while it cooks.)

Purée the celeriac in batches in a blender or food processor. Return the purée to the saucepan and add the stock and the cream. Heat but do not boil.

Take the anchovies out of their oil and chop finely. Add them to the soup. Stir in the finely chopped celery leaves, season to taste, and serve.

Chicken with Grapes

SERVES 6

WORKING TIME: 15 minutes preparation time. 30 minutes cooking time.

2 tablespoons oil
2 tablespoons lemon juice
6 boned chicken breasts
2 glasses dry white wine
50 g/2 oz mushrooms
Salt and freshly ground black pepper
2½ tablespoons flour
300 ml/½ pt White Stock (see page 127)
200 g/7 oz seedless grapes
1 tablespoon chopped basil

Melt the oil in a sauté pan and mix in 1 tablespoon of lemon juice. Take the skin off the chicken breasts and sauté them gently in the butter and lemon. Add the white wine.

Turn the chicken breasts over from time to time and don't let them brown. When they are nearly done, peel the mushrooms and stir into the dish. Add salt and pepper to taste.

Take the chicken breasts and mushrooms out of the pan and arrange them on a serving dish. Cover the dish and put it in a low oven to keep warm. Meanwhile, make the grape sauce.

Sieve the flour over the liquid in the pan and stir it in, making sure there are no lumps. Add the remaining tablespoon of lemon juice and the White Stock.

Wash and split the grapes and add them to the sauce. Heat until the grapes are warm. Pour the sauce over the chicken and garnish with chopped basil. Serve immediately.

Haricot Beans with Almonds

SERVES 6

WORKING TIME: 10 minutes preparation time. 30 minutes cooking time.

750 g/¾ lb haricot beans
1 clove garlic
1 piece lean bacon
2 tablespoons butter
75 g/3 oz blanched almonds
Salt and freshly ground black pepper

Wash, top and tail the beans and peel the garlic. Put 600 ml (1 pt) water in a saucepan with the bacon and the garlic. Bring it to the boil.

Put the beans into the boiling water and boil them rapidly without covering the pan. Cook until they are tender-crisp.

While the beans are cooking, melt the butter in a frying pan. Add the almonds, salt generously, and allow to brown.

Remove the bacon and the garlic. Drain the liquid from the beans and transfer them to a serving dish. Mix in the almonds (which should be nicely crisp) and serve.

Sautéed Spinach and Fennel

SERVES 6

WORKING TIME: 10 minutes preparation time. 8–10 minutes cooking time.

1 small bulb fennel
1 tablespoon sunflower oil
1 clove garlic
Salt and freshly ground black pepper
900 g/2 lb spinach
1 tablespoon lemon juice
1 teaspoon paprika

Wash the fennel and, if necessary, remove the outer leaves of the bulb. Dice the fennel and put it in a saucepan with just enough water to cover. Cook until the fennel is soft, 5 or 6 minutes. Drain thoroughly.

Heat the oil in a frying pan. Crush and add the clove of garlic. Dry the fennel on paper towels, then add it to the frying pan. Season to taste with salt and pepper.

Wash the spinach and put it into a saucepan over a medium heat. It should take no more than 2 or 3 minutes to become soft. Season with the lemon juice and paprika. Cut the spinach coarsely and put it in a serving dish. Top with the fennel and serve.

Cherry Frascati

SERVES 6

WORKING TIME: 15 minutes preparation time.

2 × 400 ml/14 fl oz tins black cherries in syrup
2 tablespoons Kirsch
450 ml/¾ pt Chantilly Cream (see page 142)
2 tablespoons grated dark chocolate

Drain half the syrup from the tins of cherries. In a bowl, add 2 tablespoons of Kirsch to the cherries and the remaining syrup. Poach them gently over a low flame for 5 minutes. Remove them from the heat and allow to cool.

Put the cherries in a bowl, or individual glasses, cover with the Chantilly Cream and sprinkle the grated chocolate on top.

AT thirteen, I was sent to a public school and disliked it intensely. I was six-foot two and found no one who shared my interest in cooking and poetry. I was writing or reading poetry in every spare moment. The school had a good, commonsensical, English Puritanical approach to poetry – it was handed out as a punishment by the ten or fifteen lines. These were to be learned by heart and recited to the prefects while standing on the table in their common-room.

I was tall, gawky and thin and I knew my fees were not being paid. I also knew from Keats that 'the only means of strengthening one's intellect is to make up one's mind about nothing – to let the mind be a thoroughfare for all thoughts. Not a select party'.

So I decided it was time to leave. In order not to cost my mother extra fees for not giving a term's notice, I told the Bursar at the beginning of the summer term that I should be leaving at the end of it. I think my mother was really very relieved. Fourteen-and-a-half was school leaving age in those days, so I was just within the law.

I found digs in Blackheath and worked first in Lewisham and then for the Poplar Borough Council, Baths and Washhouses department. I started attending evening school at Goldsmith's College and joined a drama group which was putting on '*The Cradle Song*'. I played 'The Chorus'. From my landlady, Emmie Shepherd and her husband Will, I learned a great deal about life on the Isle of Dogs at the turn of the century and between the wars. I also learned about nourishing, frugal food. A fellow clerk at the Baths advised me to give in my notice and 'go and act'. I joined the Burke Onwin Players in Deal.

It was a fallow time for the cooking. But, one way or another, I learned enough to get myself a job in the kitchens of the Regent's Palace Hotel when, later on, I was out of work as an actor.

MENU 7

OEUFS À LA PERIGORDINE

VEAL BIRDS PROVENÇAL

GREEN BEANS LYONNAISE

CARAMEL PEARS

Oeufs à la Perigordine

SERVES 6

THIS recipe can be eaten hot or cold. The cold eggs sliced and put on top of a terrine are quite delicious.

WORKING TIME: 20 minutes preparation time. 10 minutes cooking time.

6 hard-boiled eggs
4 teaspoons tinned pâté truffé
1 tablespoon chopped parsley
½ teaspoon chopped chervil
Salt and freshly ground black pepper
1 egg white
1 tablespoon oil

Hard-boil the eggs, then let them cool. Cut off the pointed ends and take out the yolks. Finely chop the herbs. In a bowl mash the yolks with the pâté, the herbs and the salt and pepper. Refill the whites with the mixture.

If you are planning on eating the eggs cold that is all you need to do. But if you are to eat them à la Perigordine – then whip the egg white. Heat the oil in a frying pan. Roll each egg in the beaten white and fry them lightly, turning them frequently. Put them on a warm serving dish and sprinkle the rest of the parsley over them. Serve hot.

Veal Birds Provençal

SERVES 6

WORKING TIME: 30 minutes preparation time. 45 minutes cooking time.

300 g/11 oz diced bacon
2 tablespoons chopped parsley
½ teaspoon chopped tarragon
½ teaspoon chopped basil
½ teaspoon chopped thyme
2 cloves garlic, crushed
Salt and freshly ground black pepper
6 slices of veal, thinly cut and flattened
100 g/4 oz butter
300 ml/½ pt White Stock
(see page 127)
5 tablespoons Madeira

Put the diced bacon, the chopped parsley, tarragon, basil, thyme and crushed garlic in a bowl and mix them together. Add salt and pepper to taste. Spread some of the mixture on each slice of veal. Roll it up and tie with string. Repeat with all the slices.

Melt the butter in a sauté pan and cook the veal birds until they are nicely browned on all sides. Add the stock to the veal, cover the pan and cook for 30 minutes. (You may need to add more stock during the cooking.)

Take the veal birds out of the pan and remove the string. Arrange them in a serving dish and keep warm.

Add the Madeira to the gravy in the pan. Simmer for a minute or two and stir so that all the juices are absorbed. Pour the gravy over the veal birds and serve.

Green Beans Lyonnaise

SERVES 6

WORKING TIME: 15 minutes preparation time. 25 minutes cooking time.

900 g/2 lb green beans
1 medium-sized onion
1 teaspoon parsley
100 g/4 oz butter
Salt and freshly ground black pepper
½ teaspoon lemon juice

Cut the ends off the beans and wash them. Peel and chop the onion and finely chop the parsley.

Put the beans into boiling salted water; cook until they are tender-crisp. Drain and dry them on a cloth.

Melt half the butter in a pan and sweat the onion until tender. Add the beans to the onion. Cut in the rest of the butter and sauté until the beans are beginning to brown slightly. Add a little salt and pepper to taste and finish with the lemon juice.

Turn into a dish and sprinkle with finely chopped parsley.

Caramel Pears

SERVES 6

WORKING TIME: 15 minutes preparation time. 25 minutes cooking time.

6 firm Conference pears
2 tablespoons butter
100 g/4 oz caster sugar
300 ml/½ pt double cream

Preheat the oven to 230°C/475°F/Gas mark 8. Peel the pears, cut them into quarters and core them.

Put the quarters into a baking dish. Pack the pieces closely, side by side, and rub each pear slice with a little butter. Sprinkle liberally with sugar.

Put the dish into the hot oven until the sugar turns light brown, basting with the juice of the pears.

When the sugar is caramelised pour in the cream. Mix the cream with the sugar and serve hot.

Spring

IN the summer of 1949 I got my call-up papers. I was told to stand by to go at any moment. Though I was between jobs at the time, there was a very good chance of me getting a job as Assistant Stage Manager/Understudy at the St James's Theatre, London. I was really counting my chickens and thought I was going to break into the big time; but when the Stage Director heard that I was waiting for my call-up he turned me down.

I was really very badly off and needed money desperately. Quite by chance I met an actor I knew in the Strand. He was off to work in the kitchens of the Savoy. I asked him how he got the job. 'Denmark Street Catering Exchange.' I wasted no time but cut through Covent Garden very quickly. They had a job going as a relief kitchen clerk at the Regent's Palace Hotel. Did I speak French, they asked me. 'Enough', I lied.

I was interviewed by the kitchen clerk who needed someone to take over while he went on holiday. The job was to stand behind the hotplate, take the orders from the waiters and call them in French to the chefs. You then had to make sure that the right waiter got the right order. In those days it was a very big restaurant and it was nothing to serve 500 lunches, usually in the space of a couple of hours.

I was taken on at a salary of £5.00 a week, very good money. I worked beside the clerk for a week and then he went off on holiday.

Another of my duties was to get the day's menu from the Head Chef and make copies of it. Long before Rank stepped into the lists with Xerox, kitchens had their own copiers. You filled a large baking tin with consommé and let it set. You wrote the menu for the day with an indelible pencil and pressed the page face down on to the consommé. That was your master copy. You could then take copies by putting a blank sheet of paper on the consommé and lifting it off.

It was the days of the five shilling limit on meals and the patrons would bribe the waiters with packets of cigarettes for bigger portions or better cuts. The waiter would then have to bargain with me and the chefs. So I didn't have to buy any cigarettes. After the kitchen clerk came back from his holiday I was kept on and worked in various capacities until I was called up three months later.

MENU 1

YOGHURT SOUP WITH PRAWNS

BAKED TROUT IN HONEY AND LEMON

PURÉE OF SPRING GREENS

NEW POTATOES IN PARSLEY BUTTER

COMPOTE OF ORANGES IN PORT

Yoghurt Soup with Prawns

SERVES 6

WORKING TIME: 30 minutes preparation and cooking time.

1.5 litres/2 pt yoghurt (either Homemade Yoghurt (see page 141) or bought live yoghurt)
1 tablespoon cornflour
Salt and freshly ground black pepper
600 ml/1 pt prawns
600 ml/1 pt White Stock (see page 127) or potato water
1 clove garlic
¼ teaspoon fenugreek
1 tablespoon chopped fennel green

Stabilise the yoghurt so that it doesn't curdle. To do this put the yoghurt in a saucepan and beat it thoroughly until it is liquid. Mix the cornflour with 2 tablespoons of water, or enough to make it smooth, and add it to the yoghurt. Stir in ½ teaspoon of salt and bring the yoghurt to the boil, stirring gently all the time in one direction only. Just as it begins to boil, turn the heat down and let it sit on the heat, barely simmering, for about 10 minutes. It will begin to thicken very nicely.

In another saucepan heat the stock. Chop the prawns in a blender or food processor and add them to the stock. Crush the garlic and add to the stock, together with the fenugreek.

Now gently pour the yoghurt on to the stock stirring all the time in the same direction. Don't let the soup boil. Sprinkle with chopped fennel greens and serve.

Baked Trout in Honey and Lemon

SERVES 6

WORKING TIME: 1–2 hours marinating time. 15 minutes preparation time. 15 minutes cooking time.

6 small cleaned trout
3 tablespoons honey
3 tablespoons lemon juice
½ teaspoon powdered cumin
Pepper
2 tablespoons oil

Put the trout into a shallow dish. Pour the honey and the lemon juice over them and sprinkle with powdered cumin and pepper to taste. Cover the dish with greaseproof paper and let it stand.

To cook, take each trout out of the marinade and lay it on greaseproof paper. Pour a little oil over it and wrap it up. Put the fish on a flat baking tin and cook for 15 minutes in a 180°C/350°F/Gas mark 4 oven.

Purée of Spring Greens

SERVES 6

WORKING TIME: 20 minutes preparation time. 10 minutes cooking time.

800 g/1¾ lb spring greens
1 onion
2 tablespoons sunflower oil
1 tablespoon lemon juice
150 ml/¼ pt Vegetable Stock (see page 128) or water
Salt and freshly ground black pepper
2 tablespoons butter

Wash the greens, cut out the centre stalk and chop them.

Peel and slice the onion and heat the oil, lemon juice and some of the Vegetable Stock or water in a saucepan. Cook the onion in it until it is soft. Pour in the rest of the stock and bring to the boil. Add the greens and cook until tender, about 5 minutes.

Pour off the water and transfer the greens and onion to a food processor or blender and purée.

Season with salt and pepper to taste. Put the purée back into the saucepan and reheat with a little butter. Transfer the purée to a serving dish and serve immediately.

New Potatoes in Parsley Butter

SERVES 6

WORKING TIME: 25 minutes preparation and cooking time.

900 g/2 lb new potatoes
Sprig of mint
Salt and freshly ground black pepper
2 tablespoons butter
2 tablespoons chopped parsley

Wash and scrub the new potatoes. Put them into a saucepan with enough boiling water to cover. Add a sprig of mint and salt to taste. Cook for 15 minutes or until the potatoes are ready when tested with a fork. Pour off the water (which may be kept for stock).

Put the potatoes back in the pan and cover them with a cloth for a moment to dry them. Put the butter into the pan and roll the potatoes round in it. Turn out on to a hot serving dish and sprinkle the chopped parsley over them.

Compote of Oranges in Port

SERVES 6

THIS dish can be prepared in advance. In fact it's nicer if kept chilled for a day.

WORKING TIME: 30 minutes preparation and cooking time. 3 hours cooling time, at least.

4 oranges
100 g/4 oz sugar
300 ml/½ pt port
2 teaspoons lemon juice
Rind of 1 lemon
¼ teaspoon cinnamon
300 ml/½ pt whipped cream

Peel the oranges, making sure that you remove the pith. Slice them and remove the pips.

Boil up the sugar and 150 ml (¼ pt) water in a saucepan until it become syrupy. Add the oranges and all the other ingredients; boil gently for 2 or 3 minutes.

Take the oranges out of the pan and arrange them on a serving dish. Boil down the liquid until it thickens and pour it over the oranges, cool them and then chill. (This recipe can be made up to this point and then kept up to 24 hours).

When the oranges are ready to be served top with whipped cream. (Use double or whipping cream. When it is fluffy, stir in a teaspoon of lemon juice.)

THE army is used to coping with and absorbing misfits. I was sent to the Rifle Brigade for my initial training. Within three months they had squared me up, put me through a War Office Selection Board and sent me off to Aldershot to be commissioned in the Tank Regiment.

It was a brisk six months. I went to my first Derby, was involved in a car crash and concussed. I spent some days in St Thomas's hospital then was given ten days' sick leave and hitch-hiked to France. On that convalescent trip I saw Edith Piaf performing 'live' and walked for miles all over Paris. I ate very cheaply and realised that there is a fundamental difference in the approach to food on either side of the Channel. They do love it so and take such pleasure in it.

On my return I met a film costume designer, Julia Squire. She had just been given her first big film to design, David Lean's *The Magic Box*. I was commissioned at the beginning of December 1950 and we married on the 22nd.

Soon afterward the Army posted me to Hong Kong. The Regiment was stationed up in the New Territories, quite a long way from Kowloon. I have never been suited to an all male environment; I find it quite unnatural. However, I was made Equitation Officer and was able to ride off into the foothills on most afternoons.

Up in the hills there was a monastery which seemed to be an open order judging by the women, children, dogs and chickens that lived there. The monks were very hospitable and I was allowed to sit there quietly and read. On one occasion I was invited to share their rice and vegetables, which I did with great pleasure. I also had the great good fortune to be befriended by a Chinese lawyer and his family who had a weekend house in the foothills. Here I spent some very happy Sundays eating all sorts of delicacies, pork meat balls with waterchestnuts, and crabmeat, lobster, steamed duck, and pork with cheese, which, in concept, was like the Bulgarian pork fillet with cheese stuffing, but much more delicate in execution. I love eating Chinese food but have never really tried to cook it.

After that exotic interlude I was shunted down to the R.A.C. Ranges in Pembrokeshire to finish my National Service. The ranges were only used in the summer and this was autumn and winter. I made friends with farmers on the perimeter of the ranges. One was a very good shot, so I ate a lot of pheasant, wild duck and snipe. Since there was no Officers' Mess at the camp, I persuaded the Commanding Officer to let me have a living-out allowance. I quite often had leftover meat from game, chicken or ham. I learnt to make crêpes as the best way to deal with the problem. I still find a ham and chicken filling quite the nicest.

MENU 2

DOLMAS

HAM AND CHICKEN CRÊPES

GLAZED CARROTS

BROCCOLI WITH MUSHROOM

PEPPERMINT ICE CREAM

Dolmas

SERVES 6

WORKING TIME: 30 minutes preparation time. 2 hours cooking time.

200 g/7 oz preserved vine leaves
1½ cups long grain rice
3 tomatoes
1 onion
4 cloves garlic
2 tablespoons finely chopped dill
1 tablespoon finely chopped mint
¼ teaspoon fenugreek
Salt and freshly ground black pepper
150 ml/¼ pt olive oil
Juice of 1 lemon

You will need to get the salt out of the preserved vine leaves. To do this, put them in a bowl and pour boiling water over them. Separate the leaves so that the water can get between them. Soak for 20 minutes, drain them and then soak them in fresh cold water for 2 or 3 minutes. It's advisable to do this several times.

While the vine leaves are soaking, cook the rice. I usually allow 1½ cups of boiling water to 1 cup of rice. (A lemon quarter added to the water and cooked with the rice is very good.) Bring the water and the lemon to the boil in a saucepan, then add the cup of rice. Cover and allow to boil for 4 or 5 minutes. Take the lid off the saucepan and continue to simmer until the rice is done. Transfer it to a sieve and wash it in cold water. Leave it to cool.

Skin and chop the tomatoes. Peel and chop the onion and 1 clove garlic and chop the dill and mint. Stir these ingredients into the rice and add the fenugreek, salt and pepper to taste.

Put a vine leaf on the work board, the veins of the leaf uppermost. Put a spoonful of the rice mixture onto the leaf, fold the stalk end of the leaf over first then fold in the sides and roll it into a neat sausage. Continue stuffing the leaves until you have used all the filling.

Line the bottom of a saucepan with rinsed vine leaves, and pack your dolmas very tightly into the pan, layering them. Peel the remaining garlic and put the whole cloves on the dolmas about a layer from the top. Pour in the oil, the lemon juice and 150 ml (¼ pt) water. Weight down the dolmas with a plate or round dish that fits your pan, otherwise they may unroll.

Cover the pan and simmer very gently for about 2 hours. Check occasionally in case you need to add more water.

Drain the dolmas, cool them and serve cold. Serve garnished with lamb's lettuce, chopped red peppers and half a lemon. The combination of colours is very attractive.

Ham and Chicken Crêpes

SERVES 6 (ABOUT 20 CRÊPES)

THIS recipe is deliciously useful when you have some chicken and ham to use up.

WORKING TIME: 1 hour preparation and cooking time. 2 or more hours cooling time for crêpes.

FOR THE CRÊPES

200 g/7 oz sifted flour
½ teaspoon salt
3 eggs
400 ml/¾ pt milk
150 ml/5 fl oz sunflower oil

FOR THE FILLING

350 g/12 oz leftover cooked ham and chicken
600 ml/1 pt Melted Butter Sauce (see page 132)
3 teaspoons Dijon mustard
Salt and freshly ground black pepper
2 teaspoons lemon juice
2 tablespoons melted butter
100 g/4 oz grated cheese

Put the flour, eggs and salt into a food processor and blend. Add the milk slowly. Make sure that there are no lumps. Finally, add the oil. Allow the mixture to stand for about 2 hours.

Give the batter a good stir before cooking the crêpes. Heat up a heavy frying pan without any grease or oil. When the pan is hot, drop 1½ tablespoons of the batter at a time into the pan. There is quite enough oil in the batter to cook it. Tilt and rotate the pan so that the batter evenly covers the bottom. It should be thin, so it will only need about 1 minute on each side.

Heat a soup plate over a saucepan of hot water. Keep the crêpes warm on it.

Put the ham and chicken in a food processor or blender and chop. Add the Dijon mustard and lemon juice to the Melted Butter Sauce. Salt and pepper to taste. Stir the chopped ham and chicken mixture into the sauce.

Preheat the oven to very hot: 240°C/475°F/Gas mark 9. Fill each crêpe with some of the mixture and roll it up. Put the crêpes into a lightly greased baking dish, pour a little melted butter over them and then sprinkle with grated cheese.

Put the crêpes in the oven for about 45 minutes or as long as it takes to brown them. Serve immediately.

Glazed Carrots

SERVES 6

WORKING TIME: 35 minutes preparation and cooking time.

450 g/1 lb plump new carrots
2 tablespoons sugar
60 g/1½ oz butter
½ teaspoon salt

Wash and peel the carrots. If they are too big, cut them in half, lengthways.

Put the carrots in a large sauté pan. The carrots should have plenty of elbow room. Add the other ingredients and bring to the boil. When the water is boiling fast turn down the heat and cover the pan. Simmer until the liquid has nearly evaporated. Roll the carrots round in the pan so that they are well covered with the syrup, and serve.

Broccoli with Mushrooms

SERVES 6

WORKING TIME: 15 minutes preparation and cooking time.

350 g/12 oz broccoli
100 g/4 oz mushrooms
2 cloves garlic
2 tablespoons butter
1 tablespoon chopped parsley
300 ml/½ pt White Stock (see page 127)
Salt and freshly ground black pepper

Wash the broccoli and prepare by cutting the stalk to 5 cm (2 in). Bring 300 ml (½ pt) water to the boil in a saucepan. Put the broccoli in a steamer, set it over the boiling water and steam for about 8 minutes or until the broccoli is tender.

Peel and chop the mushrooms. Melt the butter in a saucepan, peel the garlic and crush it into the butter. Stir in the chopped parsley and the chopped mushrooms. Cook for 3 minutes, then add the White Stock and seasoning to taste.

Put the steamed broccoli into a serving dish and pour the mushroom sauce over it.

Peppermint Ice Cream

SERVES 6

WHEN you come to serve this lovely ice-cream, you might like to melt a 225 g/ 8 oz block of dark chocolate over some hot water, and add a small glass of Creme de Menthe to it. Pour a little over each serving of ice cream.

WORKING TIME: 30 minutes preparation time. (Make several hours ahead to chill.)

2 tablespoons sugar
2 egg yolks
½ teaspoon peppermint essence
750 ml/1¼ pt whipped double cream

Boil the sugar and 150 ml (¼ pt) water together and allow to evaporate until it becomes syrup. If you put a metal spoon into the mixture it should form a thread as you take it out.

Put the egg yolks into a bowl and beat the syrup into them a little at a time. Add the peppermint essence. Beat until you have a creamy mousse. Fold in the cream, put in the freezer, and keep until frozen.

MY brother-in-law, Raglan Squire, was kind enough to manufacture a job for me in his architect's office while I found an acting job. Julia was working on John Huston's film *The Moulin Rouge* in Paris. I was able to go over on two occasions because Rag's office needed drawings and blueprints collected or taken over.

We made many friends on that production. Among them was Louis Fleury, who was to have a great influence on my culinary life. His family had been hoteliers of great note for many years and there seemed to be no restaurant in France that Louis did not know and where he wasn't known and loved. He took us to one of his favourites, Chez Jacques, off the Boulevard Raspail. It was his favourite on two counts, firstly because of the food and secondly because Monsieur Jacques had managed to send him food parcels all the time he was a prisoner of war.

A French Cavalry Division had charged an advancing German Panzer Division in 1940. Louis took his men into the battle with a drawn sword, against the German tanks. He spent five years as a prisoner of war, so it was not surprising that Chez Jacques was the first restaurant he visited after his release.

The Poulet à l'Estragon was sensational.

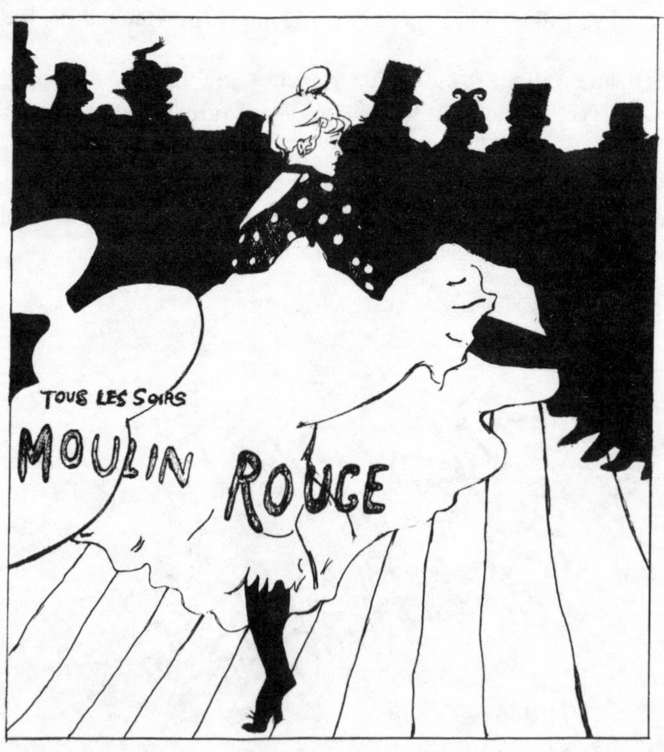

MENU 3

SMOKED SALMON ROLLS

POULARD À L'ESTRAGON

MANGETOUT WITH GRAPES

MASHED POTATOES

(see page 14)

AVOCADO PARFAIT

Smoked Salmon Rolls

SERVES 6

YOU can make this recipe some hours in advance. It should be eaten chilled but not too cold.

WORKING TIME: 35 minutes preparation time. (This can be made several hours ahead of time and chilled.)

575 g/1¼ lb white fish (cod or haddock)
300 ml/½ pt milk
1 teaspoon nutmeg
100 g/4 oz soft goat's cheese
1 tablespoon oil
1 tablespoon chopped fresh dill
Salt and freshly ground black pepper
175 g/6 oz smoked salmon

Wash and skin the fish. Put the fish, together with the milk and nutmeg, into a saucepan. Cook over a medium heat until the fish is done, about 7 or 8 minutes.

Put the goat's cheese into a bowl and soften with some of the oil. The amount of oil used will depend on the consistency of the cheese.

Drain the milk from the saucepan but keep it to one side. Mix the goat's cheese and the fish together, adding a little of the milk if the blend is too dry. Fold in the dill and salt and pepper to taste.

Form the mixture into six sausage-shaped rolls. Wrap it in slices of smoked salmon.

Poulard à l'Estragon

SERVES 6

WORKING TIME: 15 minutes preparation time. 1¼ hours cooking time.

1 roasting chicken (about 2 kgs/4½ lb in weight)
1 lemon
4 or 5 sprigs of tarragon
1 clove garlic
150 g/5 oz lean bacon pieces
900 ml/1½ pt White Stock (see page 127)
1 glass dry white wine
1 tablespoon tarragon vinegar
Salt and freshly ground black pepper
Egg Liaison (see page 132)
2 tablespoons double cream (optional)

Wash and clean the bird. Cut the lemon in half, squeeze the juice over the bird. Put the squeezed halves inside, together with the whole peeled garlic and two sprigs of tarragon.

Cut the rind off the bacon slices and put them over the breast and legs of the bird. Put the chicken into a large flame-proof casserole and add enough White Stock to cover the bird. Put another sprig of tarragon into the casserole. Chop and reserve the remainder of the tarragon for use later.

Bring the chicken to the boil, quite rapidly, and then cook gently for about 1½ hours, or until it is done. Take the casserole off the heat and remove the chicken. Remove the bacon and tarragon, and the garlic and lemons from inside. Cover the chicken and put it in a slow oven, just to keep it warm.

Remove as much of the fat from the casserole as possible by using absorbent kitchen paper. Put the casserole back on the flame and bring to the boil. Add the glass of white wine, the tarragon vinegar and season to taste. Make the Egg Liaison and add it to the sauce. Heat to a thickish consistency, but don't allow to boil, and add the cup of chopped tarragon. If you like, drop in a tablespoon or two of cream.

Pour most of the sauce over the chicken and keep some back to serve in a sauceboat.

Mangetout with Grapes

SERVES 6

WORKING TIME: 15 minutes preparation and cooking time.

575 g/1¼ lb mangetout
225 g/8 oz seedless grapes
2 tablespoons butter
150 ml/¼ pt White Stock (see page 127)
2 tablespoons lemon juice
Salt and freshly ground black pepper

Top and tail the mangetout. Wash and halve the grapes.

Put the butter, the stock and the lemon juice in a saucepan. Heat but don't boil. When the liquid is hot add the grapes. Bring to the boil and then add the mangetout for 2 minutes. Drain and add salt and pepper to taste.

Avocado Parfait

SERVES 6

WORKING TIME: Soak the apricots overnight. 30 minutes preparation time, 15 minutes cooking time.

225 g/8 oz dried apricots
1 avocado
Juice of 1 orange
Juice of 1 lemon
1 tablespoon runny honey
2 kiwi fruit
2 tablespoons double cream

Soak the dried apricots overnight. Cook them in boiling water, but no sugar. Let them cool, then mash or purée in a blender.

Scoop the flesh from the avocado and put it into a bowl. Beat in the juice of 1 orange, 1 lemon and the honey. Blend the avocado mixture with the apricot purée.

Whip the double cream, and fold it into the parfait. Top with sliced kiwi fruit. Chill and serve cold.

IT wasn't long before I got myself a job with the Salisbury Arts Theatre Company. They were playing an eight-week season in Carlisle.

I remember two plays very well for various reasons. Leslie Phillips was playing Fancourt Babberley in *Charley's Aunt*. I played Charlie Wykeham, pretty badly. Leslie was kind enough to take the time to teach me a lot about comedy. I've never really missed not going to an acting school. My years of assistant stage managing, of playing small parts and of being taught by older actors and actresses now seems to me to have been a good apprenticeship.

The other play was *Man and Superman* in which I played 'Tavy'. It was the first time I had read Shaw and I have returned to the Plays and the Prefaces constantly ever since. The director of the company was Guy Verney, who asked me to continue with them in Salisbury. He became a great friend and was to give me my first television part. I used to hitch-hike to London after the show at least every other week and cook a happy Sunday lunch.

I acquired an agent, an audition with H M Tennents, and was soon off to Manchester with *Aren't We All?*, a comedy by Frederick Lonsdale which opened some weeks later at the Haymarket Theatre, London, to a Gala Performance.

MENU 4

CHILLED FENNEL AND CRAB SOUP

ROAST LEG OF LAMB WITH LIVER PÂTÉ STUFFING

ROAST POTATOES

BRAISED CELERY

CARIBBEAN WHIP

Chilled Fennel and Crab Soup

SERVES 6

WORKING TIME: 35 minutes preparation and cooking time. Several hours chilling time.

2 fennel bulbs
2 tablespoons sunflower oil
1 tablespoon lemon juice
225 g/8 oz cooked crab meat
1.75 litres/3 pt White Stock (see page 127)
1 glass dry white wine
Salt and freshly ground black pepper
150 ml/¼ pt double cream

Wash and slice the fennel, reserving the green sprigs. Keep the core as it will go very well into a stockpot.

Put the sunflower oil and lemon juice into a saucepan and heat. Add the sliced fennel and cook until tender, slowly adding some White Stock.

Take the fennel out of the saucepan, put it into a food processor and blend it with some more of the stock until it has a smooth consistency. Return the purée to the saucepan. Add the crab meat and the remaining stock. Stir in the white wine and bring to the boil. When it is boiling turn down the heat and simmer for 10 minutes. Season with salt and pepper to taste.

Take the soup off the heat, add the cream and combine thoroughly. Chill.

Before serving, chop the green fennel leaves very finely and add to the soup.

Roast Leg of Lamb with Liver Pâté Stuffing

SERVES 6 OR MORE

WORKING TIME: 40 minutes preparation and cooking time for the pâté, 15 minutes preparation time for the lamb. Approximately 1 hour cooking time for the lamb.

FOR THE PÂTÉ

1 small onion
50 g/2 oz bacon pieces
2 tablespoons butter
1 tablespoon lemon juice
2 cloves garlic
150 g/5 oz chicken livers
¼ teaspoon nutmeg
¼ teaspoon fenugreek
Salt and freshly ground black pepper
1 tablespoon brandy

FOR THE LAMB

1 boned leg of lamb (weighing about 1½ kg/3 lb)
150 ml/¼ pt light oil
Salt and freshly ground black pepper
2 carrots
½ parsnip
2 cloves unpeeled garlic
3 or 4 large sprigs rosemary
300 ml/½ pt Brown Stock **(see page 126)**
1 glass white wine

Make the pâté. Peel and slice the onion. Cut any excess fat from the bacon pieces and cut them into small cubes.

Heat the butter and the lemon in a saucepan. Put the onion and the bacon pieces into the pan and cook until soft. Do not let the onions brown.

Peel the cloves of garlic and wash and clean the livers. Bring 150 ml (¼ pt) water to the boil in another saucepan. When the water is boiling add the garlic and livers. Cook for about 3 or 4 minutes, then drain off the water. Transfer the livers and the garlic to a food processor or blender. Add the bacon pieces and the onion. Blend to a smooth pâté.

Put the pâté in a bowl. Stir in the nutmeg, fenugreek, salt and pepper to taste. Mix in the brandy.

If you need to keep the pâté for some days, melt a little more butter and cover the pâté with it.

Ask your butcher to bone the leg of lamb for you. Tie the leg securely and oil it well. Carefully stuff the bone cavity with the pâté and fold the flaps around it. Rub in salt and pepper.

Preheat your oven to 240°C/475°F/Gas mark 9. Wash and peel the carrots and parsnip. Slice them and place in a baking dish with the rest of the oil, the cloves of garlic and the rosemary. Put the leg of lamb on top of the vegetables and roast in the hot oven.

After 10 minutes, reduce the heat slightly, continuing to do so over 30 minutes until you reach 180°C/350°F/Gas mark 4. Cook at this temperature for another 15 to 20 minutes. I like my lamb pink; my wife doesn't. Ah well, there has to be compromise in everything. Cook the lamb until it suits your taste.

Take the lamb out of the tin and put it on a serving dish, keeping it warm.

Put the baking tin on top of the oven and bring the juices in it to the boil. Pour in the glass of wine and stir into the juices. Let the sauce reduce, pour in the Brown Stock, and bring to the boil again. Sieve the gravy and pour it into a sauceboat.

Serve with the lamb.

Roast Potatoes

SERVES 6

WORKING TIME: 10 minutes preparation time. 40 minutes cooking time.

Sprig of mint
6 medium potatoes
3 tablespoons oil or butter
Salt and freshly ground black pepper

Wash, peel and halve the potatoes.

Bring 600 ml (1 pt) water to the boil, add the mint and the potatoes to it. Cook the potatoes until they are nearly done. They should be firm but cooked. Save the potato water for stock or soup.

Put the butter in a shallow baking dish and place in the oven to heat. When the butter is hot, add the potatoes. Salt and pepper them to taste and cook in a moderate oven (the lamb should by this time be down to a more moderate oven heat). Baste them occasionally, and turn them. Cook until they turn a golden-brown.

Braised Celery

SERVES 6

WORKING TIME: 20 minutes preparation time. 1 hour cooking time.

3 heads celery
225 g/8 oz carrots
1 large onion
Salt and freshly ground black pepper
600 ml/1 pt White Stock, or Vegetable Stock (see pages 127 and 128)
1 teaspoon sugar
1 tablespoon finely chopped parsley

Wash and trim the celery, cutting it down to about 15 cm (6 in). Remove the outer leaves. Cut the celery in half so that you now have 6 pieces of celery. (If you keep the leaves and trimmed ends you can add them to the potato water and make a celery soup.) Peel the carrots and slice them.

Peel the onion and chop it finely. Put the onion and carrot in a good-sized saucepan and cover with the stock. Put in the celery, salt and pepper and bring to the boil. Turn down the heat, put the lid on the pan and simmer until the celery is tender. It will take about an hour or a little more to cook. The celery should be very tender.

Remove the celery from the pan and arrange it on a serving dish. Now boil the stock in the pan until it has reduced. Stir in the sugar. When it has melted pour the sauce over the celery. Sprinkle the chopped parsley over the celery and serve.

Caribbean Whip

SERVES 6

WORKING TIME: 15 minutes preparation time.

300 ml/½ pt cold strong black coffee
2 ripe bananas
2 tablespoons rum
3 tablespoons caster sugar
600 ml/1 pt whipped cream

The coffee should be made in advance.

Peel the bananas, slice them and mix them with the rum and the sugar. Stir in the coffee.

Whip the cream, keeping a spoonful or two to one side. Fold the banana mixture into the cream.

Spoon the Caribbean Whip into ramekins or glasses and top each one with a knob of whipped cream. Chill and serve.

LIFE came fast and furious at us. *Aren't We All?* opened at the Haymarket Theatre in October 1953 and ran for six months. As soon as the play closed I played a small part in *The Intruder* with Jack Hawkins and George Cole, directed by Guy Hamilton. It was on the strength of that that I was offered an ABPC seven-year contract. The first film I did under my contract was *The Dambusters*.

I was also offered some good parts at Stratford. That's where I should have gone, but my two younger brothers needed a home and came to live with Julia and me. Suddenly, we were providing for a family.

I eagerly bought and read Elizabeth David's *Book of Mediterranean Food*. We began to entertain, and I had to learn to put menus together. As we were able to spend more money on food, I began to realise the pleasure and scope of cooking as a hobby.

MENU 5

FISH KEBABS

CHICKEN FRICASSÉ

PEPPERED BEANS

PEAS À LA FRANCAISE

GRAPE PUDDING

Fish Kebabs

SERVES 6

WORKING TIME: 1 hour preparation time. 15 minutes cooking time.

900 g/2 lb monkfish or other hard-fleshed white fish
1 glass white wine
2 tablespoons oil
1 teaspoon fenugreek
Salt and freshly ground black pepper
4 lean back bacon slices
300 ml/½ pt Homemade Yoghurt (see page 141)
1 teaspoon cornflour
1 tablespoon milk
1 tablespoon chopped mint

Wash and clean the fish. Cut it into cubes about 2.5 cm (1 in) thick.

Put the wine, half the oil, the fenugreek and salt and pepper into a shallow dish. Marinade the fish for 20 minutes or so.

Cut the rinds off the bacon slices, then cut the bacon into small squares. Put the pieces of marinaded fish onto skewers, alternating the fish with pieces of bacon. Cook under a hot grill.

Stabilise the yoghurt by mixing 1 teaspoon cornflour with a little cold milk and a little salt. Beat the yoghurt in a saucepan until it is liquid. Add the cornflour mixture and stir with a wooden spoon. Bring the yoghurt to the boil, stirring constantly in one direction. As soon as the yoghurt has boiled, turn down the heat so that the yoghurt is barely simmering. It will now take on a smooth, thick consistency. Mix in the chopped mint.

Take the fish and bacon off the skewers and arrange attractively on separate plates. Pour the sauce over them and serve.

Chicken Fricassé

SERVES 6

WORKING TIME: 30 minutes preparation time. 45 minutes cooking time.

1.4 kg/3 lb spring chicken
1 tablespoon sunflower oil
1 clove garlic
1 tablespoon flour
2 glasses dry white wine
300 ml/½ pt White Stock (see page 127)
4 or 5 mushrooms
2 shallots
1 tablespoon fresh chopped tarragon and basil
2 egg yolks
3 tablespoons double cream
1 tablespoon lemon juice
1 teaspoon Dijon mustard
Salt and freshly ground black pepper

Bone the chicken. Slice the breast of chicken and the brown meat from the legs into servable portions.

Put the oil into a flameproof dish big enough to take the chicken pieces in one layer. Heat the oil over medium heat and crush the garlic into the oil. Add the chicken pieces and brown them. Sprinkle flour over them; pour over the white wine and the White Stock.

Peel the mushrooms and boil them in a little water for 4 or 5 minutes. Put the mushrooms to one side, but add the mushroom liquid to the saucepan. The chicken pieces should now be covered with liquid. If they are not, add a little more water. Chop the shallots and the herbs and add them to the dish.

Cover the dish and cook in a 180°C/350°F/Gas mark 4 oven, for about 30 minutes, or until the chicken is tender. Take the chicken pieces out of the dish and put them into another dish to keep warm. Return the sauce to a hot flame and reduce to about half.

Beat the yolks of egg into the cream. Take the sauce off the heat and thicken it by adding the cream mixture to it quite slowly. Add the juice of lemon, and the Dijon mustard. Season with salt and pepper to taste. Strain the sauce, reheat it – making sure it doesn't boil – and pour it over the chicken.

Peppered Beans

SERVES 6

WORKING TIME: 10 minutes preparation time. 10 minutes cooking time.

800 g/1¾ lb French beans
Salt and freshly ground black pepper
2 tablespoons butter

Cut the stalks off the beans. Boil 600 ml/1 pt salted water in a saucepan and drop the beans in. Turn down the heat a little. Let them boil, but not fiercely, for about 10 minutes, or until tender.

Drain off the water, reserving it for stock. Put the drained beans back on the heat to make sure that all the moisture has evaporated. Add the butter and toss the beans in it. Now grind plenty of pepper on to them and serve.

Peas à la Francaise

SERVES 6

WORKING TIME: 10 minutes preparation time. 35 minutes cooking time.

1 small lettuce
8 or 9 small new onions
1 teaspoon chopped parsley
1 teaspoon chopped chervil
800 g/1¾ lb shelled peas, fresh or frozen
75 g/3 oz butter
Salt and freshly ground black pepper
1 teaspoon sugar

Shred the lettuce into fine strips. Peel and chop the onions. Wrap the herbs in a small piece of muslin.

Put the prepared peas into a saucepan with the lettuce, chopped onion and herbs. Cut the butter into small pieces and add that to the pan. Pour in 150 ml (¼ pt) water and the sugar. Add salt and pepper to taste.

Bring the peas to the boil very gently, then reduce the heat and simmer for about 20 minutes. Remove the bouquet garni and drain the peas. Return to the saucepan. If you think the vegetables need a little more butter stir in an extra teaspoon. Serve.

Grape Pudding

SERVES 6

WORKING TIME: 30 minutes preparation and cooking time.

250 ml/8 fl oz Homemade Yoghurt (see page 141)
225 g/8 oz seedless grapes
75 g/3 oz soft brown sugar

Wash and dry the grapes, remove all stems and peel them. Mix them with the Homemade Yoghurt. Spoon the grape mixture into a shallow dish and press them down. Sprinkle the brown sugar over them and chill in the fridge.

SOON after *Dambusters* I was tested by John Huston for a part in *Moby Dick*. There were about eight of us who were tested; none of us got the part. John Huston got the actor he had always wanted, Richard Basehart.

But at the instigation of his secretary, Jeanie Sims, Huston gave me a copy of the test I had made for him. It earned me my first starring role in pictures in *The Ship That Died of Shame* with Richard Attenborough. For a time I was a 'hot property', as they say. I did a film at Shepperton and one at Pinewood.

Julia had just given birth to our first daughter, Candy. I had time for a short holiday between films and, as it was not possible to take Julia and Candy with me, I went alone.

I went to Paris and consulted Louis Fleury. There were two or three things I wanted to do; I wanted to go to Avignon and see the Palace of the Popes, to go to Arles and the Camargue and see where Van Gogh painted, and visit Bandol, where Frieda took D. H. Lawrence to find a miracle cure for his T. B., and to Vence where he died. I had with me the poems of D. H. Lawrence and the *Cantos* of Ezra Pound.

Louis gave me my gastronomic itinerary over the most splendid meal of Canard aux Olives at Vincent Allard's restaurant. I went there again a couple of years ago. It is now run by his sons but the duck was as delicious as I had remembered.

My first port of call was to be the Relais Fleury at Pouilly-sur Loire. I was to have the Ecrevisses à la Creme. Madame La Laitre supposed I knew what I was talking about, or guessed that I didn't, and suggested the most superb lunch. I was drinking a glass of marc with her when her husband, a jovial, red-faced man, came in with two cronies, also jovial red-faced men. It transpired that one was the Grand Vigneron de Pouilly and the other the Chef de Caves du Chateau Nozet. They decided that I must taste some of their superb wine. I was supposed to reach Lyons that night but I was told it was essential for me to see the game between Pouilly and somewhere or other the next afternoon. I drank a great deal of the wine of the region and discovered that the French were not only crazy about cycling but fanatical about basketball. I arrived forty-eight hours adrift in Lyons, but I treasure the memory of bucketing about the N7 in a deux chevaux with those three formidable drinkers. Pouilly Fumé is still one of my favourite wines.

MENU 6

LEMON CHICKEN SOUP

SHRIMP-STUFFED GREEN PEPPERS IN SAUCE CRÉOLE

GRILLED TOMATOES WITH FENNEL

TARRAGON-LEMON MUSHROOMS

APPLE PEPPERMINT

Lemon Chicken Soup

SERVES 6

WORKING TIME: 15 minutes preparation time. 1¼ hours cooking time (This timing assumes that you are starting from scratch and making the chicken stock from a new carcass).

1 chicken carcass, with giblets
4 stalks celery, leaves and all
4 cloves garlic
2 lemons
¼ teaspoon fenugreek
Salt
Paprika
175 g/6 oz cooked rice
1 small lettuce finely chopped

Remove the meat from the carcass. Put the carcass and giblets in a pan with the celery. Add 2 litres (3½ pt) water. Chop the garlic and add that to the pan. Cut 1 lemon in half and put the 2 halves into the pan, together with the fenugreek.

Bring the soup to the boil, remove the scum from the surface, then turn down the heat, cover the pan and simmer for about an hour. Remove the soup from the heat and strain through a fine sieve.

Lay absorbent kitchen paper across the top of the soup to remove any fat. Pour the liquid back into the pan, add salt and paprika to taste and the juice of the other lemon. Stir in the rice and the finely chopped lettuce, return to the heat for 5 minutes, and then serve.

Shrimp-Stuffed Green Peppers in Sauce Créole

SERVES 6

WORKING TIME: 20 minutes preparation time. 35 minutes cooking time. The rice and Sauce Créole (page 136) can be prepared a day or two before you need them.

6 green peppers
1 shallot
1 tablespoon chopped bulb fennel
225 g/8 oz cooked rice
225 g/8 oz cooked shrimps
225 g/8 oz mozzarella cheese
Sauce Créole (see page 136)

Cut the tops off the peppers and remove the seeds and ribs. Put the peppers in a pan of boiling water, then turn down the heat and simmer for 10 minutes or until the peppers are just tender. Drain them on absorbent kitchen paper and let them cool for a few minutes.

Chop the shallot and grate the cheese.

Preheat the oven to 180°C/350°F/Gas mark 4. Put the rice, the fennel and the shrimps in a bowl. Mix together thoroughly and stuff the peppers with the mixture. Put them upright in a baking dish.

Pour Sauce Créole over each one and sprinkle with chopped shallot and mozzarella cheese. Put the peppers in the oven and cook for about 20 minutes. The cheese should be nicely melted and the peppers hot.

Grilled Tomatoes with Fennel

SERVES 6

WORKING TIME: 15 minutes preparation time. 15 minutes cooking time.

9 firm tomatoes
100 g/4 oz chopped bulb fennel
4 tablespoons butter
Salt
Paprika
1 tablespoon chopped parsley

Cut the tomatoes in half and remove the seeds with a teaspoon. Finely chop the fennel and sauté it in a little butter until tender. Add salt and paprika to the fennel and mix in the chopped parsley.

Put a little of this stuffing into each of the seeded tomatoes. Top with a dot of butter on each and grill until hot and bubbling.

Tarragon-Lemon Mushrooms

SERVES 6

WORKING TIME: 15 minutes preparation and cooking time.

675 g/1½ lb open mushrooms
2 tablespoons butter
2 tablespoons lemon juice
2 teaspoons sugar
1 tablespoon tarragon vinegar

Peel and wash the mushrooms. Heat the butter and lemon juice in a pan. Add the sugar and the mushrooms and cook until they are just soft. At the last minute stir in the vinegar. Serve immediately.

Apple Peppermint

SERVES 6

THIS can be made the day before you need it and kept in the fridge.

WORKING TIME: 15 minutes preparation time. 20 minutes cooking time.

3 medium cooking apples
1 teaspoon lemon juice
1 tablespoon sugar
2 tablespoons cream
1 teaspoon butter
200 g/7 oz bitter cooking chocolate
Peppermint essence

Peel and core the apples. Slice them roughly, then place in a saucepan with the lemon juice and sugar. Stew until lumpy. When the apples are cooked, beat in 1 tablespoon of cream. Divide the apple mixture into six ramekins.

Melt the butter in a saucepan. Break up the chocolate and melt that with the butter. Add the second tablespoon cream and a few drops of peppermint essence. Pour some chocolate over each of the ramekins. Allow to cool until the chocolate has hardened.

IT was during the 1975 R.S.C. season at Stratford that I first heard of pippins and caraway.

HENRY IV, PART II, Sc III.
Gloucestershire. The Garden of Shallow's House.

Enter. Falstaff, Shallow, Silence, Bardolph, the Page, and Davy.

SHALLOW: Nay, but you shall see mine orchard, where, in an arbour, we will eat a last year's pippin of my own graffing, with a dish of caraways, and so forth; come, cousin Silence; and then to bed.

FALSTAFF: 'Fore God, you have a goodly dwelling, and rich . . .

SHALLOW: Barren. Barren, barren; beggars all, beggars all, Sir John; marry, good air. Spread, Davy; spread, Davy . . . by the mass, I have drunk too much sack at supper.

I couldn't believe that the caraway was sprinkled on the Cox Pippin and that was that. It couldn't be so simple. I found the answer in Florence White's *Good English Food*:

> Roasted apples eaten with caraway comfits are an early eighteenth-century preventative of many of the ills that flesh is heir to.

And again;

> Apples are apt to cause flatulence, for which caraway seeds and comfits give relief, and it was the custom of our ancestors to serve a dish of baked apples and caraway comfits after a meal.

I was obviously on to something here. I thought it would be wonderful to make some comfits. This time I found my answer in Florence White's *Good Things in England*. She quotes from Charles Elme Francatelli:

> The manufacture of comfits embraces various very complicated processes. It forms in itself a special branch of confectionery . . .

I was very quickly persuaded that I was not going to be making caraway comfits. The utensils required, the time it would take and the absolute certainty of failure sent me scurrying off to find another method of tasting 'Pippins and Caraway'.

Caraway is the most versatile seed; it can be used with cabbage, carrots, rice, as tea, in cakes and bread, in pickles, with fish, in jams, and, of course, in comfits.

MENU 7

EGGS EN COCOTTE WITH TARRAGON

VEAL THOMAS JEFFERSON

SPINACH RICE

BAKED APPLES AND CARAWAY

Eggs en Cocotte with Tarragon

SERVES 6

WORKING TIME: 30 minutes preparation and cooking time.

2 teaspoons butter
6 eggs
Salt and freshly ground black pepper
300 ml/½ pt White Stock (see page 127)
4 or 5 sprays of tarragon

Butter 6 ramekins and break the eggs into them. Season with salt and pepper.

Pre-heat the oven to 230°C/450°F/Gas mark 8. Pour some boiling water into a baking dish, put the ramekins into it and cook in the oven for about 7 minutes.

Put the tarragon (reserving some leaves for decoration) and the White Stock into a pan and reduce the liquid. Pour the reduced liquid over the eggs through a sieve. Decorate the ramekins with tarragon leaves and serve immediately.

Veal Thomas Jefferson

SERVES 6

WORKING TIME: 40 minutes preparation time. 20 minutes cooking time.

300 ml/½ pt Sauce Bearnaise (see page 133)
6 × 100 g/4 oz veal cutlets
900 g/2 lb of fresh asparagus
1 clove garlic
1 glass dry white wine
Juice of 1 lemon
1 tablespoon flour
Salt and freshly ground black pepper
50 g/2 oz butter
800 g/1¾ lb crab meat
25 g/1 oz shrimps

Prepare the Sauce Bearnaise in advance, and keep warm in a bain-marie.

Ask your butcher to pound the veal into thin pieces.

Cook the asparagus in boiling, salted water. Drain and keep warm. Crush the garlic and put it in a bowl with the white wine and the lemon juice. Dip the veal into this mixture. Sprinkle the flour lightly on to the veal, and season with salt and pepper to taste.

Melt the butter in a sauté pan and sauté the veal for about 5 or 6 minutes, turning it over once or twice. Put it aside to keep warm. Gently warm the crab meat under a low grill.

Warm the Sauce Bearnaise in a bain-marie.

Put the veal on a serving dish. Pour some sauce over each escalope, then a layer of crab meat. Cover that with asparagus, put a few shrimps on top as garnish, and serve.

Spinach Rice

SERVES 6

THIS recipe uses Basmati or other white rice. If you wish to use brown rice, the same quantities apply but the cooking time will be longer. If you wish you can add butter and lemon to taste.

WORKING TIME: 30 minutes preparation and cooking time.

FOR THE RICE

2 cups rice to 3 cups water
½ lemon
Salt and freshly ground black pepper

FOR THE SPINACH

575 g/1¼ lb spinach
1 tablespoon oil
Salt and freshly ground black pepper

Put the water in a pan and bring to the boil. Add the rice and the half lemon. Cover the pan and allow it to boil for about 4 minutes. Turn down the heat and uncover the pan, stirring periodically to allow the water to evaporate. Season with salt and pepper.

Wash the spinach well and remove the stalks. Put 300 ml (½ pt) water into a pan and bring it to the boil. Put the stalks into the boiling water and cook for about 4 minutes until tender. Drain, pouring the pan water into a bowl, to keep for stock.

Pour the oil into the pan, heat it, and toss the spinach in it. Season with salt and pepper. Purée the spinach in a food processor or blender.

To make the Spinach Rice, mix the rice and spinach together.

Baked Apples and Caraway

SERVES 6

WORKING TIME: 35 minutes preparation and cooking time.

6 large Cox Pippins
2 tablespoons caraway seeds
2 tablespoons raisins
1 tablespoon lemon juice
1 small glass Calvados
2 tablespoons clear honey

Wash and core the apples and arrange them on a baking tray.

Push a few raisins, some caraway seeds, a little of the lemon juice and Calvados into the cored apples. Pour honey over each apple and sprinkle with the rest of the caraway seeds. Bake in a preheated 180°C/350°F/Gas mark 4 oven for about 25 minutes.

Summer

I believe very few people would associate Noel Coward with Yorkshire Pudding, but he was a dab hand at it.

'The batter for a Yorkshire pudding should be allowed to stand some time in the cool, and shouldn't be mixed with milk – instead use a little salted water. Lift the beef onto the rack above the baking tin and let the juices drip down on to the pudding,' he told me. He paused for a moment. 'Brown, crisp and utterly delicious,' he added.

I first met Noel in 1958 at one of the shortest interviews I've ever had. I went to the Dorchester hotel to meet him about appearing in his play *Look After Lulu* which was to be put on in New York. I walked through the door, he looked at me and said, 'Oh yes, fine'. He turned to his secretary and said, 'Ring Cyril in New York and tell him the part is cast'. Two weeks later I was on my way to New York.

Although the play was not a critical success, we ran for five months. Noel became a great friend and many years later when I was running a theatre company at Bury St Edmunds he came to a gala night to see a performance of *Private Lives*.

It was thirty-three or four years after he had written the play and he was greatly moved when the audience stood up and applauded him with shouts of 'Author'.

The night before coming to Bury he was at the Comedy Theatre seeing a mutual friend, Richard Leech. It was when Richard said, 'I hear you're going to see George' that Noel made one of his splendid remarks. 'Yes, I go to Bury not to praise him.'

All this has really nothing to do with summer cooking but recalling it sparked the memory of a meal I had with Noel in New York. I give it for my first summer menu.

MENU 1

GAZPACHO

FILETS DE BOEUF WITH SAUCE CHAUDFROID

MANGETOUT AND SHALLOTS

GRAND MARNIER SOUFFLÉ

Gazpacho

SERVES 6

WORKING TIME: 30 minutes preparation time. (This soup should be made at least 2 to 3 hours in advance).

6 cloves garlic
3 tablespoons stale white breadcrumbs
600 ml/1 pt White Stock (see page 127)
4 tomatoes
1 cucumber
4 peppers (green and red)
1 glass dry white wine
Salt and freshly ground black pepper
600 ml/1 pt single cream
2 slices white bread, crusts removed
2 tablespoons light oil
1 tablespoon chopped chervil leaves

Crush the garlic and put it in the food processor with the stale breadcrumbs. Blend thoroughly. Put the breadcrumbs and garlic mixture into a bowl. Stir in sufficient stock to make it a smooth paste. Continue to add the rest of the stock.

Wash and peel the tomatoes. Put 2 of them into the blender and 2 to one side. De-seed the cucumber. Put half of it in the blender and reserve half. Wash, de-seed and de-rib the peppers, keeping 2 to one side and putting the other 2 into the blender. Add the glass of white wine. Season with salt and pepper and blend the vegetables to a smooth paste. Stir the blended vegetables into the bread and garlic chicken stock.

Bring the cream to the boil, leave it to cool and then blend it into the stock. Allow the soup to chill for at least 2 to 3 hours.

Chop the remaining vegetables and put them into separate bowls to be served with the soup. Dice the bread and fry the cubes in the hot oil to make croûtons. Add a spoonful of each of the chopped vegetables, some croûtons and chervil to the bowls of soup before serving.

Filets de Boeuf with Sauce Chaudfroid

SERVES 6

WORKING TIME: 1½ hours preparation, cooking and standing time.

900 g/2 lb fillet of beef
4 tablespoons butter
300 ml/½ pt Sauce Chaudfroid (see page 138)
1 hard-boiled egg white
300 ml/½ pt Aspic Jelly (see page 140)
4 cold mashed potatoes
100 g/4 oz cooked green peas
1 tablespoon double cream
Salt and freshly ground black pepper

Trim all the skin and gristle from the fillet. Cut the fillet into 6 equally-sized rounds, about 1 cm (½ in) thick. Melt the butter in a steak pan and fry the fillets until they are browned outside but pink inside, about 3 minutes each side. Put the cooked fillets between two plates and place a weight on top to flatten them. (I usually use a saucepan of water as a weight). Leave them to cool.

Trim the edges of the fillets if you need to. Cover with the Sauce Chaudfroid and let them set. Chop up the hard-boiled egg white and sprinkle a little on top of each fillet. Pour some half-set Aspic Jelly over.

Make 6 small mounds of cold mashed potato on a serving dish and arrange a fillet on each, leaving a space between the fillets.

Pass the cooked peas through a sieve and then blend them with the cream. Season to taste with salt and pepper. Put this purée into a piping bag and decorate around each fillet. Chop up the rest of the aspic and garnish the serving dish.

Mangetout and Shallot

SERVES 6

WORKING TIME: 25 minutes preparation and cooking time.

425 g/1 lb mangetout
1 small shallot
100 g/4 oz seedless grapes
1 tablespoon oil
2 teaspoons lemon juice
Salt and freshly ground black pepper

Wash and remove the stalks from the mangetout. Peer the shallot and chop it finely. Wash and cut the seedless grapes in two.

Put the oil and the lemon juice into a pan, heat, and cook over a low heat until soft.

Put the mangetout in a basin and pour some boiling water over them. Let them stand for a few seconds, then drain. Put them into the pan with the onion. Add ½ glass of water. Boil the mangetout for about 3 minutes. Add the grapes and continue to cook for another minute or two. Season with salt and pepper to taste. Drain off any remaining liquid. Allow to cool and serve with a vinaigrette dressing.

Grand Marnier Soufflé

SERVES 6

WORKING TIME: 30 minutes preparation and cooking time.

8 egg whites
225 g/8 oz sugar
6 egg yolks
2½ tablespoons plain flour
450 ml/¾ pt milk
150 ml/¼ pt Grand Marnier

Beat the egg whites in a large bowl until stiff. Stir in 4 tablespoons of the sugar while continuing to beat the whites. Put them in the fridge.

Combine the egg yolks, the flour and the rest of the sugar in a bowl, then mix in the milk. Whisk the mixture until smooth. Sieve the mixture into a saucepan, then heat it over a moderate flame until it begins to thicken. Stir in the Grand Marnier. Let it stand until it is lukewarm.

Butter a soufflé dish and sprinkle it with a little sugar. Put the mixture into it and gradually fold in the egg whites. Cook in a hot oven for 12 minutes.

A series of seemingly unrelated events led to my being invited to stay with an American lawyer, his wife and large family in their beautiful house overlooking the Hudson River and Brooklyn Bridge. In 1957 I was doing a TV serial, *The Truth About Melandrinos* in Birmingham. I rented a cottage in the Cotswolds, so that the family could be with me, and commuted to work.

Unexpectedly I was called to London and, as I was not needed in the studio the next day, I decided to stay the night. My friend, Richard Leech, rang and asked me if I was free to come to dinner and help entertain an elderly American friend. I thoroughly enjoyed dinner and the company of Edna Chappell. The next day I returned to Birmingham and work.

A friend who was going through a painful divorce was staying with us for the weekend. We went for a drive around the villages on Saturday evening and called in for a drink at The Lygon Arms, Broadway, before going home. Down the stairs and into the bar came Edna Chappell, her daughter Joan and her son-in-law, Cuz Hardee. They were touring the Cotswolds. I asked them to come and spend Sunday with us and we spent a charming day sightseeing. We got through a lot of food and a lot of drink amid a lot of laughter. Joan was crippled with polio and had lost the use of her arms but managed brilliantly and the little help she needed Cuz gave her so unobtrusively as not to be noticed. Before they left Cuz gave me their New York address and asked me to phone if I ever came to America.

Three months later I arrived in New York to start work on *Look After Lulu*. After a few days I rang the Hardees who were incensed that I was staying at an hotel. They insisted I check out and stay with them in Brooklyn Heights.

At this time they had five children, four between them and one of their own. Joan managed her life in the nursery and the kitchen with her feet. The kitchen had been adapted so that every appliance could be controlled by foot. She even steered her car by foot. I enjoyed the expressions of other drivers as we swept through New York with the steering wheel apparently doing its own thing.

One night, just before the play opened, I was invited to a party, where I was introduced to Tallulah Bankhead, who wanted to talk about London. When she found out that we were opening the next night she spat in my eye for luck. We have many extraordinary traditions in the theatre: 'Break a leg' is supposed to be terribly lucky; 'Merde' say the French, with an encouraging smile. Tallulah Bankhead spits in your eye. This is, luckily, quite an uncommon form of wishing you luck.

MENU 2

MUSHROOMS À LA GRECQUE

MEAT LOAF WRAPPED IN BACON

If you are going to eat it hot:

NEW POTATOES
(page 40)

FRENCH BEANS

If you are going to eat it cold:

TOMATO AND ONION SALAD

CUCUMBER AND YOGHURT SALAD

CHERRY TART

Mushrooms à la Grecque

SERVES 6

WORKING TIME: 30 minutes preparation and cooking time. (This is best if prepared a day ahead.)

350 g/12 oz button mushrooms
3 tablespoons olive oil
2 cloves garlic
4 tablespoons chopped parsley
Juice 1 lemon
Salt and freshly ground black pepper

Peel the mushrooms. Pour the olive oil and 1 tablespoon water into a frying pan and heat. Crush the garlic and stir it into the pan with the chopped parsley. Add the lemon juice.

Bring the liquid to the boil, then add the mushrooms. Let them simmer until they are tender, about 10 minutes. Turn the contents of the pan out onto a dish to cool – allow as much as one day. Add salt and pepper to taste before serving.

Meat Loaf Wrapped in Bacon

SERVES 6 OR MORE

IF you are feeling particularly generous, you could use half best mince and half entrecôte steak.

WORKING TIME: 1 hour 15 minutes preparation and cooking time.

2 small onions
1 clove garlic
2 teaspoons capers
1 tablespoon chopped mint
1 tablespoon chopped parsley
1 teaspoon chopped dill
1 teaspoon chopped basil
800 g/1¾ lb best mince
1 teaspoon Dijon mustard
2 lemons
Salt and freshly ground black pepper
225 g/8 oz long back green bacon

Peel the onions. You can chop the onion, the garlic, the capers and the herbs in a food processor. Put the mince into a bowl and mix the chopped ingredients into the meat. Add the mustard and the juice of a lemon. Season with salt and pepper.

Preheat the oven to 190°C/375°F/Gas mark 5. Cut the rind off the bacon. Take a good-sized piece of aluminium foil and lay some greaseproof paper on it. Arrange the bacon slices on the paper, thin end to thick end alternately. Shape the meat into a loaf, place it over the bacon slices, and wrap them around it. Cut the other lemon into quarters and arrange them round the loaf.

Wrap the foil tightly around the meat and lemon quarters. Put the loaf into a baking dish and bake for about 30–35 minutes.

French Beans

SERVES 6

WORKING TIME: 30 minutes preparation and cooking time.

675 g/1½ lb French beans
1 shallot
1 tablespoon sunflower oil
1 tablespoon lemon juice
2 tablespoons butter
Salt and freshly ground black pepper

Bring 900 ml/1¾ pt water to a rapid boil in a saucepan. Add the beans and cook them for about 5 minutes. Drain, rinse the beans under cold water and set them aside. Peel and finely chop the shallot. Pour the sunflower oil and lemon juice into a frying pan. Add the chopped shallot and cook for 3 to 4 minutes. Stir in the beans and the butter and cook for another 5 minutes. Sprinkle the salt and pepper to taste and stir. Serve immediately.

Tomato and Onion Salad

SERVES 6

WORKING TIME: 10 minutes preparation time.

6 tomatoes
1 medium onion
1 tablespoon sunflower oil
Salt and freshly ground black pepper
2 tablespoons tarragon vinegar
1 tablespoon chopped parsley

Slice the tomatoes thinly and peel and chop the onion finely. Put the tomatoes in a serving dish and sprinkle the onions over them.

Pour the oil over the tomato and onion, then season with salt and pepper. Sprinkle over the vinegar, follow with the parsley, and mix.

Cucumber and Yoghurt Salad

SERVES 6

WORKING TIME: 30 minutes preparation time. (Ideally, this should be made the day before and left to stand in the fridge.)

1 medium cucumber
1 teaspoon salt
1 clove garlic
300 ml/½ pt Homemade or 'live' Yoghurt (see page 141)
1 teaspoon sweet paprika

Thinly slice the cucumber. Put the slices on a plate and sprinkle them with salt. Cover with another plate and let the cucumber weep; this will take about 15 minutes.

Drain off the surplus water and put the cucumber in a serving dish. Crush the garlic into a bowl and mix in the cucumber. Stir in the cup of yoghurt and sprinkle with the paprika. Chill and serve.

Cherry Tart

MAKES A 23 CM (9 IN) TART

WORKING TIME: 1¼ hours preparation time for the pastry. 40 minutes preparation and cooking time for the tart.

FOR THE PASTRY:

225 g/8 oz flour
150 g/5 oz butter
1 egg
100 g/4 oz caster sugar
1 or 2 drops vanilla essence

FOR THE FILLING:

400 g/14 oz stoned cherries
300 ml/½ pt double cream
1 egg yolk
2 teaspoons sugar

Sieve the flour in one bowl and cream the butter in another. Quickly mix the flour and butter together in the larger bowl.

Make a well and add the egg, the caster sugar, the drops of vanilla essence and 2 teaspoons of water. Blend the ingredients together, as quickly and lightly as possible.

Roll the pastry into a ball and let it stand in a cool place for an hour.

Roll out the pastry to fit a 23 cm (9 in) tart tin. Line the tart tin with the pastry. Fill it closely with the stoned cherries.

In a bowl, whip the cream and the yolk of egg together. Sprinkle the cherries with the sugar. Pour the whipped cream and egg over the cherries and bake in a preheated 190°C/375°F/Gas mark 5 oven for about 25 minutes.

NEW York was magical. There were poets and musicians to appreciate, places to see and a new culture to absorb. Earlier I had been surprised, when being shown the University of Moscow, to see that they had a Faculty for English Language and a Faculty for American Language. Of course, we had seen Tennessee Williams' *Street Car Named Desire* and Arthur Miller's *Death of a Salesman*, but that did not prepare me for poets like Ginsburg and Ferlinghetti or for the music in Birdland.

Nor were the English doing too badly in New York. The Old Vic was drawing full houses on Broadway and there were three or four English actors starring in Broadway plays. But dominating the scene was John Gielgud in *The Ages of Man*. Tickets were like gold dust. I was lucky to get one.

I was waiting for the curtain to rise when a young woman and her rather older escort came in to occupy the seats next to me. It soon became clear that they were father and daughter and that she was there under duress. The buttoned-up face told its own story. She wasn't going to like Shakespeare. But the genius of the writer and the actor prevailed and I saw her laughing with Benedick and crying with Lear. Her hand stole into her father's during the second half of the show and I felt the tension lift from his shoulders.

I came back from New York, my cases bulging with records and poems. Dill bread quickly became a favourite with the family – when you could find the dill. Neither mangetout nor basil were easily procurable then, but they are now. The mixture is irresistible.

MENU 3

HERBED BREAD

SALMON CASSIS

CASSOULET OF VEAL AND HARICOT BEANS

MANGETOUT WITH BASIL

DAMSON JAM ICE CREAM

Herbed Bread

SERVES 6 OR MORE

HERB or garlic breads are easy to prepare and go so well with certain dishes. Garlic bread goes particularly well with red meats, fennel bread with fish, and dill bread with omelettes and white meat.

WORKING TIME: 10 minutes preparation time. 15 minutes cooking time.

1 or 2 French loaves
Butter
2 cloves garlic per loaf
or
1 heaped tablespoon chopped fresh fennel or dill

Split the loaf lengthwise and butter each side generously. Then force the garlic cloves through a press and spread the crushed garlic over the buttered bread, or if using the fresh fennel or dill, spread that over, reaching all the edges. Press the cut halves together, wrap tightly in aluminium foil, and heat through for 15 to 20 minutes in a preheated 180°C/350°F/Gas mark 4 oven. Unwrap and cut the bread into large hunks to serve.

Salmon Cassis

SERVES 6

YOU can use the ordinary canned blackcurrants you find in the supermarket for this sophisticated – and extremely simple – *hors-d'oeuvre*.

WORKING TIME: 15 minutes preparation time.

450 g/1 lb middle cut of salmon
2 teaspoons lemon juice
Salt and freshly ground black pepper
225 g/8 oz blackcurrants in syrup

Remove the skin from the salmon. Put it raw into a blender or food processor and purée it finely. Transfer the salmon purée to a bowl and add the lemon juice, salt and pepper to taste. Add a little of each at a time to arrive at the taste you prefer.

To make the cassis dressing, put the blackcurrants, syrup and all, through the blender or food processor, then pass the purée through a fine sieve. Put a large spoonful of the salmon purée on each plate, and surround with a thin pool of the cassis dressing. Garnish the plate with chopped green salad and cucumber.

Cassoulet of Veal and Haricot Beans

SERVES 6

THIS cassoulet can be made the day before as it improves with re-heating.

WORKING TIME: 30 minutes preparation time. 1½ hours cooking time.

225 g/8 oz dried haricot beans
3 onions
4 cloves
900 g/2 lb veal pieces
90 g/3½ oz flour
2 tablespoons sunflower oil
1 tablespoon lemon juice
2 glasses dry white wine
4 tablespoons chopped parsley
Salt and freshly ground black pepper

Soak the dried haricots overnight.

Put them in a pan (I always use the water they were soaked in to cook them). If there is insufficient water add enough to cover generously.

Peel the onions. Stick the cloves in one of the onions and add that to the haricots. Bring the beans to the boil and skim off the scum. Turn down the heat and allow to simmer for about an hour.

Trim the veal pieces and roll them in flour. Slice the remaining onions.

Put the sunflower oil and the lemon juice in a frying pan. Heat, then add the onions. Let the onions cook until softened and lightly coloured. Add the veal pieces, and brown for 15 minutes. Transfer the veal to a cassoulet or casserole dish. Drain the haricots, add them to the veal, and pour in the wine. Put in half the parsley. Salt and pepper to taste.

Put the lid on the cassoulet. Slide it into a preheated 180°C/350°F/Gas mark 4 oven. Cook for about 1 hour. Just before serving sprinkle over the remaining parsley.

Mangetout with Basil

SERVES 6

WORKING TIME: 10 minutes preparation and cooking time.

675 g/1½ lb mangetout
1 tablespoon sunflower oil
2 teaspoons lemon juice
1 clove garlic
2 tablespoons chopped basil
Salt and freshly ground black pepper

Wash and trim the mangetout. Bring 6 cups of water to the boil. When the water is boiling rapidly, add the mangetout and cook for about 30 seconds. Drain and rinse in cold water. Reserve.

Into a sauté pan put the sunflower oil, the lemon juice and the crushed garlic. Cook for a minute or two, then add the chopped basil and the mangetout.

Turn up the heat and toss rapidly until the mangetout are heated through. Salt and pepper to taste. Serve immediately.

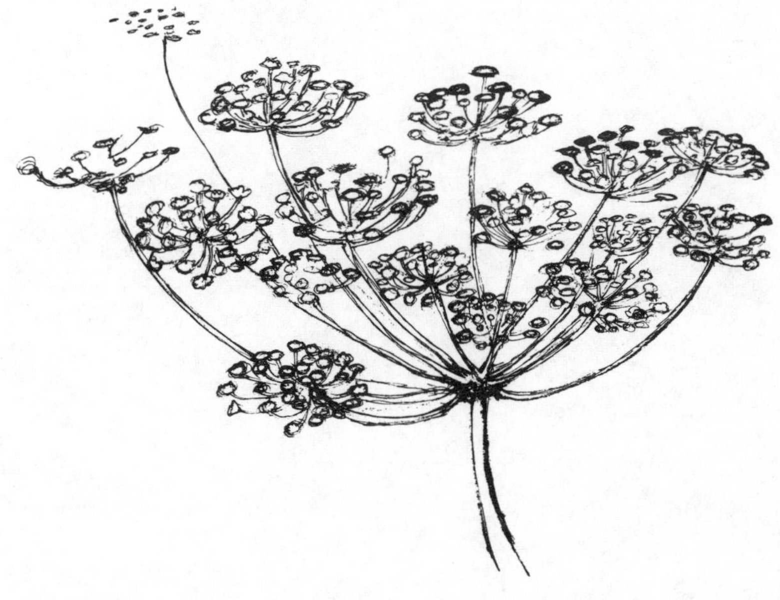

Damson Jam Ice Cream

SERVES 6

AS a child I saw the harvesting of roses in Bulgaria. The petals are used for rose oil which is exported for use in perfumes. They are distilled for rose water and used for making preserves. I use rose petals when I make my own damson jam. Rosepetal syrup sounds very esoteric but if you have roses in your garden or can get hold of some rose petals it's well worth a try.

WORKING TIME: 20 minutes cooking time. 8–24 hours freezing time.

2 tablespoons sugar
750 ml/1¼ pt double cream
2 eggs
½ teaspoon vanilla essence
2 tablespoons damson jam

Boil the sugar together with 750 ml (1¼ pt) water to make a syrup. (A good way of testing that the syrup is ready is by dipping a metal spoon into it and seeing if it forms a thread when you bring it out.) Whip the cream and put into the fridge. Separate the eggs. In a large bowl whip the whites. Chill them in the fridge. Put the egg yolks into a bowl. When the syrup is ready, beat it a little at a time into the yolks. Add the vanilla essence. Beat the mixture into a creamy mousse. Fold in the cream.

Make sure that there are no stones in the damson jam, then beat it into the cream. I use an electric hand whisk. Lastly, fold in the whites. Pour the mixture into a dish and freeze.

A FEW years ago I went to Australia to film a sequence for a corporate video I was producing. I went through Sydney so that I could spend some days with my daughters, Candy and Charlie, both now Australians. Candy is a journalist currently writing for the *Melbourne Age*. She has also published three *Yacker* books of interviews with Australian writers who are working at home and abroad. Charlie is a chef who has now stepped out of the kitchen into management.

The night before I left for Melbourne, Charlie gave a dinner party for me. Candy and her friend, Robert Drewe, were both there. Robert is, arguably, one of Australia's best novelists. The dinner was splendid but Charlie had excelled herself with the Cold Stuffed Spatchcock. I give her recipe in this menu.

After Charlie and I had washed up, I packed ready for my early start to Melbourne. I walked the few yards to Rushcutter Bay. Suddenly I became aware of a group of young people crossing a bridge some yards away from me. I thought it time to go home, but not soon enough. In a twinkling I was surrounded by six young men with knives. One knocked my glasses off and cut my nose. 'We're not joking,' he said. Another dug his knife into my kidneys. I didn't think it was the moment to be brave. I simply asked them to spare me my cards.

The police were not very impressed. As one of the detectives put it, 'It was a good thing you had the money on you or there's no way they wouldn't have used the knives.' What made the event quite bizarre was that behind a screen in the police station the television was playing an old film of mine *The Moonraker*, in which I swash-buckled myself out of danger against all odds. Reality isn't half as much fun.

MENU 4

TOMATO, BASIL AND MOZZARELLA SALAD

COLD STUFFED SPATCHCOCK

SWEET-AND-SOUR COURGETTES

MIXED GREEN SALAD

SUMMER PUDDING

Tomato, Basil and Mozzarella Salad

SERVES 6

WORKING TIME: 15 minutes preparation time.

6 large tomatoes
3 packets mozzarella
3 tablespoons chopped basil
Whole basil leaves
2 tablespoons olive oil
4 tablespoons lemon juice
Salt and freshly ground black pepper

Slice the tomatoes and mozzarella thinly. Arrange the slices of tomato and mozzarella alternately on 6 small plates. Sprinkle the chopped basil over the salad. Lay some of the whole basil leaves as a garnish on the plates.

Mix the oil and lemon; season with salt and pepper to taste. Pour the dressing over each salad before serving.

Cold Stuffed Spatchcock

SERVES 6

WORKING TIME: 2 hours preparation and cooking time.

3 spring chickens, weighing about 275 g/10 oz each.
3 small eggs (you can use gull's eggs, guinea fowl eggs, bantam eggs or just small chicken eggs)
275 g/10 oz leaf spinach
200 g/7 oz feta cheese, drained
Salt and freshly ground black pepper
3 tablespoons sunflower oil
1 glass white wine

Bone the chickens. Do this by putting the chickens breast-side-down on a board and cutting the length of the backbone. Cut off the pinions and the feet at the joints. Cut away the flesh from each side of the carcass and remove the carcass. You can then detach the thigh bones from the inside of the meat. The birds are then ready for stuffing.

Hard-boil the 3 eggs and preheat the oven to 190°C/375°F/Gas mark 5.

Wash and cook the spinach in as little water as possible, or steam it. When it is cooked, drain it well and put it through the blender with the drained feta cheese. The mixture you require is quite a solid paste.

Put some of the cheese and spinach mixture into the boned chicken. Salt and pepper to taste. Shell the hard-boiled eggs and put one on each chicken. Place it at the breast of the bird to help you return the chicken to its original shape. Sew the back of the chicken up with a needle and cotton. Brush the birds with the oil. Roast in the moderately hot oven for 30 minutes or until golden brown.

While the chickens are cooking, break the carcasses into pieces and boil them up in 300 ml (½ pt) water and a glass of white wine. Allow this mixture to reduce to one-third its volume and remove the bones. Set it to one side.

Remove the spatchcock from the oven and allow them to cool a little before covering them with the demi-glaze. Serve cold.

Sweet-and-Sour Courgettes

SERVES 6

WORKING TIME: 10 minutes preparation time. 15 minutes cooking time.

675 g/1½ lb courgettes
2 shallots
1 tablespoon olive oil
1 tablespoon malt vinegar
1 tablespoon lemon juice
1 tablespoon soy sauce
2 tablespoons honey
½ teaspoon fenugreek powder
Salt and freshly ground black pepper

Wash and slice the courgettes. Bring 300 ml (½ pt) water to boil in a pan. When the water is boiling rapidly, drop the courgettes into it. Cook for about 3 minutes. Drain the courgettes and set aside.

Finely chop the shallots. Heat the oil and the vinegar in a saucepan and cook the shallots in it until tender. Stir in the lemon juice, soy sauce, honey, fenugreek and seasoning. Finally add the courgettes and cook for another 3–5 minutes.

Allow to cool for at least 2 hours.

Mixed Green Salad

SERVES 6

I ONCE read a theory that the delicate leaves of lettuce are easily bruised, so coating them first with oil prevents the salt, vinegar or lemon from damaging them.

WORKING TIME: 15 minutes preparation time.

1 lettuce
1 curly endive
1 head chicory
¼ cucumber
1 green pepper
1 tablespoon chopped dill
2 tablespoons sunflower oil
Salt and freshly ground black pepper
1 tablespoon lemon juice

Wash all the salad ingredients and drain thoroughly.

Mix the lettuce leaves and curly endive in a bowl. Slice the head of chicory crosswise, separate the rings, and add them to the bowl. Slice the cucumber as thinly as possible and core, deseed and rib the pepper. Cut it into rounds. Add both to the salad, together with the chopped dill.

Pour on the sunflower oil. Toss the salad so that the leaves are lightly coated with oil. Season with the salt and pepper. Finally, add the lemon juice and toss the salad again.

Summer Pudding

SERVES 6–8

WORKING TIME: 10 minutes preparation time. (Let it stand overnight.)

450 g/1 lb raspberries
150 g/5 oz redcurrants
100 g/4 oz sugar
Slices of 1 or 2 day-old white bread
Cream (optional)

Stew the fruit and sugar in a pan for about 3 or 4 minutes in order to make the juices flow. Take off the heat and leave to cool.

If you use sliced bread, it should definitely be 2 days old. Slice the bread and cut off the crusts.

Line the bottom and the sides of an old-fashioned pudding basin with the bread slices, reserving some for the top. It's important that there should be no gaps. Fill up with the fruit but reserve most of the juice. Cover the top with slices of bread.

Put a plate or flat-bottomed dish on top of the pudding and weight it down. Leave it overnight in the fridge.

Turn the summer pudding on to a plate just before serving. Pour the reserved juice over it. Serve with cream, but let each guest choose to eat this delightful pudding on its own if they want to.

IN the winter of 1961 the Old Vic went to Moscow. The plays we took were *St Joan*, *Macbeth* and *The Importance of Being Earnest*. No 'glasnost' then; we were firmly in the Kruschev era.

On the night of our arrival I went for a walk. I kept to straight lines so that I would easily find my way back to the Ukrinia Hotel. I crossed the river and walked up a hill at the top of which there was a church ablaze with lights. People were hurrying in, large cars arriving, but there were no bells ringing. I joined the crowd and went in. An Orthodox service was about to begin. Memories of my childhood in Bulgaria came flooding back to me. The singing was magnificent, the spectacle breathtaking. Later, I asked the interpreter about the Church in Russia. She told me that there were some religious services but only for the old and those infirm in mind. Most of the churches were simply kept as museums.

The next night we opened with *St Joan* to rapturous applause and standing ovations. Barbara Jefford was the toast of the town, the critics were glowing in their praise and we made the front page of *Izvestia*. The American ambassador asked the English ambassador if the British had made some sort of trade deal with Russia. We were fêted, televised and shown around the city. There were

never-ending receptions and an awful lot of vodka was drunk as we toasted each other and each other's country.

Mr Kruschev came to see *The Importance of Being Earnest.* He sat in the box and his translator spoke our lines loudly in his ear as soon as we had finished them. It was a very disconcerting experience, but Nikita had a good laugh and thoroughly enjoyed the play.

As I was in all three productions I had very little time off. Barbara Jefford and John Moffat were in the same plight. However, our Intourist guide managed to get us tickets to the Bolshoi opera the day before we left for Leningrad. *Cosi Fan Tutti* was not written for Russian voices – there was not a Mozartian note between them. But the theatre is breathtaking.

I also managed to get our interpreter to take me to a Russian restaurant – the best restaurant in Moscow, she told me. I had no way of judging that but the food was good. We started with Piroshki and then sent on to Kavkaski Shasslik.

MENU 5

PIROSHKI

KAVKASKI SHASSLIK

BOILED BROWN RICE

LETTUCE SALAD WITH SOUR CREAM

COMPOTE OF FRESH FIGS

Piroshki

SERVES 6

WORKING TIME: 40 minutes preparation and cooking time.

Unsweetened brioche dough, enough for six dariole moulds (For brioche dough see Brioche of Salmon Pâté, page 12)

225 g/8 oz cream cheese
75 g/3 oz creamed butter
3 eggs
¼ teaspoon nutmeg

Salt and freshly ground black pepper

Butter the moulds and line them with the brioche dough, reserving some for later use.

Mix the cream cheese and the butter together. Beat the eggs and add them to the cheese and butter mixture. Season with salt, pepper and nutmeg.

Fill the moulds with the mixture and cover with a thin layer of brioche dough. Leave the piroshki to rise at room temperature and away from draughts, for about 1 hour.

Cook in a preheated 220°C/425°F/Gas mark 7 oven. Turn out and serve immediately.

Kavkaski Shasslik

SERVES 6

WORKING TIME: 15 minutes preparation time. 4 hours standing time. 15 minutes cooking time.

1.5 kg/3 lb loin or leg of lamb
3 onions
3 green chilli peppers
2 bay leaves
300 ml/½ pt dry white wine
300 ml/½ pt white wine vinegar
Salt and freshly ground black pepper
3 spring onions

Cut the lamb into square pieces, but don't remove the fat. Peel and slice the onions and chop the peppers.

Put all the ingredients, except the spring onions, into an earthenware pot and let stand for 4 hours – longer if it suits you. Turn the meat over in the marinade occasionally.

Take out the meat, drain it and dry it thoroughly. Chop the spring onions very finely, using as much of the green as you can, and reserve it. Grill the meat under a hot grill. Sprinkle with the spring onions before serving.

Boiled Brown Rice

SERVES 6

WORKING TIME: 15 minutes cooking time.

2 cups of brown rice to 3 cups of water
½ lemon
1 tablespoon butter
Salt and freshly ground black pepper

Bring the water to the boil in a large saucepan. Add the rice and the lemon. Cover and let the rice absorb the water.

When the water has been absorbed and the rice is tender, put the rice in a sieve and wash under cold running water.

Melt the butter in the saucepan, add the rice and re-heat, lifting the rice with a fork. Season with salt and pepper to taste.

Lettuce Salad with Sour Cream

SERVES 6

WORKING TIME: 45 minutes preparation time.

1 good-sized head of lettuce
Salt and freshly ground black pepper
2 hard-boiled egg yolks
1 teaspoon sugar
1 tablespoon malt vinegar
150 ml/¼ pt sour cream
2 teaspoons finely chopped fennel
20 slices cucumber, very thinly cut

Wash and dry the lettuce and put the leaves in a bowl. Sprinkle them with salt and put the bowl in the fridge for 30 minutes.

Mash the yolks of the 2 hard-boiled eggs in a small bowl and mix in the sugar, a little salt and a little pepper. Now mix in the vinegar and gradually stir in the sour cream, stirring continuously.

Take the lettuce out of the fridge and drain. Toss the salad in the dressing, finally adding the fennel and the cucumber. Serve immediately.

Compote of Fresh Figs

SERVES 6

WORKING TIME: 15 minutes cooking time. 2 hours cooling time, at least.

12 figs
425 g/15 oz sugar
½ teaspoon vanilla essence

Peel the figs.

Put the sugar, 750 ml (1¼ pt) water and vanilla essence into a pan and bring to the boil. When it is boiling rapidly drop in the figs. Cook them for about 3 minutes, then drain thoroughly.

Boil the syrup until it has reduced and then pour it over the figs. Allow them to cool and serve.

A chance remark, a snatch of song and your life's changed. John Moffat and I were rather homesick at one point in Moscow, sitting in our dressing room dressed as the second and third witches. John sang in a gentle voice:

'It really is a very pretty garden
And Chingford to the eastward can be seen.
If you had a rope and pulley,
You'd enjoy the view more fully.
If it wasn't for the houses in between.'

In fact, Johnny wanted to mount a proper Old Victorian Music Hall. He put the first version of it on at The Hampstead Theatre Club. I saw it there and my life changed. For the next five and a half years I was an actor/manager.

We took the Music Hall on an eight-week tour, hoping to bring it in to London. We had a wonderful cast led by John Moffat and Doris Hare. We opened in Guildford to full and enthusiastic houses. There were two highlights in the tour, the first being Bury St Edmunds. The show might have been designed for Bury's small Regency theatre. The audience took us to their hearts. There was a gala night and the audience came dressed in their Victorian finery. We were so successful that the management of the theatre asked us back for another week. They also asked me if I would set up a company to supply the theatre with plays. That's how I became an actor/manager.

The other 'highlight' was astonishingly poignant if somewhat ironic. The Nottingham Playhouse Company was on holiday and John Neville asked us to take the Music Hall there. I had been trying to get a London home for the show but all I was offered was the Saville Theatre. It was too large, it would have swamped the show. I had been forced to turn it down.

It was Saturday when I drove up to Nottingham to tell the cast the show was closing. On the way up I heard England win the World Cup on my car radio. We were all heartbroken that the show was going to end. I watched it from the back of the stalls for the last time. It was wonderful.

A lecturer at Nottingham University was appalled that a music hall should take over from the regular fare of Shakespeare and Chekhov. He had taken a group of his students to show them how barren 'low theatre' was.

At the curtain call there was a sudden commotion and young people started running down the aisle to the front of the stage. They were carrying baskets and throwing roses on to the stage. It was the students who had been brought to mock but had returned to praise. We know the story because the lecturer wrote to John a letter full of appreciation and thanks.

My present wife, Sally Home, was in that company. We had been together for some years but we didn't get married until our daughter, Sarah, was six. She was going up to bed one evening when she turned back to us and said, 'I wonder if you two would mind getting married?' 'Why?' we asked. 'It's not very nice at school and, by the way, we never have any puddings in this house.'

At about this time I whipped together a pudding that found its way on to a London menu under the name of 'Mr Scroggin's Pudding'. Andrea Leeman was running the restaurant – I didn't mind her using my pudding as I knew that one day she would have to help me with this book! It would have been worth a thousand puddings.

MENU 6

TARAMASALATA

CHICKEN IN HONEY AND CARAWAY

FENNEL IN HOLLANDAISE SAUCE

BROAD BEANS IN BUTTER

MR SCROGGIN'S PUDDING

Taramasalata

SERVES 6

WORKING TIME: 15 minutes preparation time.

2 thick slices white bread
Milk
2 tablespoons lemon juice
75 g/3 oz smoked cod's roe
(or a pot of smoked roe)
2 cloves garlic
Paprika

Cut the crusts off the bread. Soak in enough milk to make the slices very spongy. Take the bread out of the milk and let drip dry.

Put all the ingredients, except the paprika, into the blender. (If you are using smoked roe from the fishmonger you will need to take the skin off the roe first.) Blend at a high speed.

Remove the paste into a serving bowl and season to your taste with paprika. Add a little milk, if required, to make the consistency you want.

Chicken in Honey and Caraway

SERVES 6

WORKING TIME: 35 minutes preparation and cooking time.

6 chicken legs
2 tablespoons sunflower oil
Salt and freshly ground black pepper
Honey
2 tablespoons caraway seeds
2 tablespoons lemon juice

Wash the chicken legs and remove the excess fat. Trim them to the knuckle.

Put the legs in a baking dish and pour the oil over them. Season with salt and pepper to taste. Spoon some honey over each leg and sprinkle with caraway seeds.

Pour the lemon juice over the chicken pieces and cook in a preheated oven, 220°C/425°F/Gas mark 7, for about 45 minutes.

Fennel in Sauce Hollandaise

SERVES 6

WORKING TIME: 30 minutes preparation time.

3 good-sized fennel bulbs
2 tablespoons sunflower oil
Salt and freshly ground black pepper
Sauce Hollandaise (see page 139)

Cut the top off the fennel bulbs but keep the green leaves. Slice the bulbs. When you come to the root, cut and slice the fennel around it (keep the root to put into the stock pot).

Pour the sunflower oil and 150 ml (¼ pt) water in a pan and heat. Add the sliced fennel and cook until soft. Season with salt and pepper to taste.

Drain the fennel, transfer to a serving dish and cover with the Sauce Hollandaise. Serve immediately, before the sauce congeals.

Broad Beans in Butter

SERVES 6 GENEROUSLY

WORKING TIME: 25 minutes preparation and cooking time.

900 g/2 lb frozen broad beans (or 2½ kg (5 lb) fresh)
2 tablespoons butter
Salt and freshly ground black pepper
2 tablespoons chopped parsley

Bring some water to the boil in a saucepan under a steamer. Put the frozen beans into the steamer and allow to thaw and cook. Drain thoroughly and return the beans to the pan with the butter. Heat them through and season with salt and pepper to taste.

Add the parsley and shake the pan so that it coats the beans.

Mr Scroggin's Pudding

SERVES 6

WORKING TIME: 10 minutes preparation time.

300 ml/½ pt double cream
1 tablespoon sugar
3 ripe bananas
2 teaspoons lemon juice
1 tablespoon cognac
25 g/1 oz ratafias macaroons
6 lemon slices
6 cherries

Whip the double cream in a large bowl, then beat in the sugar. Slice the ripe bananas and whip them into the cream. Fold in the lemon juice and the cognac. Crumble the ratafias and fold the crumbs into the cream.

Spoon the mixture into 6 wine glasses and garnish each with a slice of lemon and a cherry. Leave in the fridge until ready to serve.

Autumn

AUTUMN has always been my favourite season. The season of 'mists and mellow fruitfulness'. So many things to be pickled and preserved.

The village and the people of Ilmington, in Warwickshire, will be preserved in my heart and my memory for the rest of my life. I joined the Royal Shakespeare Company in 1974. I was persuaded to go to Stratford by a brilliant young director, Buzz Goodbody. She asked me to play Claudius to Ben Kingsley's Hamlet. I believe she was a genius. She had a clarity of vision which never allowed her to deviate from the main purpose of theatre as she saw it, which was to tell the story. She knew her text, understood the play and respected the contribution of the actor. Her influence remains with me to this day. I paraphrase it as 'don't try to be clever, tell the story'.

During that season at Stratford I rented a cottage in Ilmington. We were to spend a great deal of time there in the next ten years. Kind friends lent us cottages at peppercorn rents, they put us up for weekends, we rented cottages on the short and the long term.

We mounted Nativity plays in the church, the R.S.C. brought its Music Hall to the village hall, we made cider, drank homemade wine, laughed prodigiously; we were made welcome. I walked a five mile circuit of the hills every morning in every season. There is nothing so beautiful as the turning leaves of Autumn or the 'Fall' as the Americans call it. It's a very good name for it. The Fall in New England is every bit as beautiful, colder perhaps. The season cries out for nice warm soups. We've always had wonderful thick soups in England, but Clam Chowder became a favourite of mine over there.

'Clam Chowder' – the very name cries out America. Yet the Romans got it from the Greeks and the Chinese looked on Yangtse clams as a delicacy in the eighth century. The American Indians dug a hole, heated some stones, strewed seaweed on them and had a clam bake. It is also said to have been 'originally a Newfoundland fisherfolk dish' and I read that the New Englanders probably got their recipe from the French settlers in Canada'. Yet another source tells me that 'the Virginians most likely got it from the English'. Wherever it comes from it's very tasty. I agree with an old English cook book that says, 'Chouder, a sea dish'.

MENU 1

CLAM CHOWDER

OSSO BUCCO À LA MILANAISE

BROCCOLI AL FRITTO

TAGLIATELLI

BLACKBERRY AND APPLE PIE

Clam Chowder

SERVES 6

WORKING TME: 1 hour preparation and cooking time.

12 large clams
225 g/8 oz streaky bacon
2 medium onions
3 medium potatoes, sliced
Salt and freshly ground black pepper
1 teaspoon butter
3 teaspoons plain flour
300 ml/½ pt single cream

Scrub the clams and put them in a pan with enough water to cover them. Bring the water to the boil and the clams will open. Strain the clams through a sieve and reserve the strained clam stock. Take the clams out of their shells and chop them finely. Keep them to one side.

Take the rind off the bacon and chop it into small pieces. Fry them in a pan until crisp and brown. Peel and slice the onions, add them to the pan and fry until tender.

Transfer the bacon and onions to a deep saucepan, add the clams, the reserved liquid, and the sliced potatoes. Bring to the boil, then lower the heat and cook until the potatoes are tender. Season with salt and pepper to taste.

Mix the butter and the flour together, making flour balls. Drop them into the chowder to thicken it, and cook, stirring until they are dissolved. Mix in the cream and serve at once in pre-heated bowls.

Osso Bucco à la Milanaise

SERVES 6

WORKING TIME: 2 hours preparation and cooking time.

1.25 kg/2½ lb veal knuckle
2 teaspoons flour
Salt and freshly ground black pepper
2 tablespoons olive oil
3 medium onions
250 ml/8 fl oz dry white wine
3 large tomatoes
1 large or 2 small cloves garlic
300 ml/½pt Brown Stock (see page 126)
Bouquet garni (or if you have them chop some fresh herbs of your choice, tie them in a piece of muslin and put it in the casserole)
Lemon juice
Chopped parsley

Cut the veal knuckle into 6 pieces. Roll them in a little flour and season with salt and plenty of black pepper. Put the veal pieces in a casserole with the olive oil and sauté until brown.

Peel and chop the onions, add these to the casserole and fry until golden brown. Pour over the dry white wine and allow this to reduce.

Peel and deseed the tomatoes, chop them coarsely and add them to the casserole. Pour in the stock and press and add the garlic. Drop in the bouquet garni. Stir the contents of the casserole to combine thoroughly.

Cover the casserole and put it in a preheated 200°C/400°F/Gas mark 6 oven for 1½ hours. Just before serving, squeeze over lemon juice to taste and decorate with chopped parsley. Serve from the casserole.

Broccoli al Fritto

SERVES 6

WORKING TIME: 25 minutes preparation and cooking time.

675 g/1½ lb broccoli florets
2 eggs
50 g/2 oz breadcrumbs
75 g/3 oz butter
Salt and freshly ground black pepper

Wash the broccoli and trim the stalks. Bring 600 ml (1 pt) water to the boil in a saucepan under a steamer. When the water is boiling rapidly, steam the broccoli, covered, for 3 minutes.

Take the broccoli florets out and dry them on a cloth. Beat the eggs. Dip the broccoli into the egg and roll the florets in the breadcrumbs. Heat the butter until it is sizzling and quickly fry the broccoli in it. Season to taste and serve.

Tagliatelli

SERVES 6

WORKING TIME: 6 to 7 minutes preparation and cooking time.

225 g/8 oz tagliatelli fresh or dried
1 tablespoon olive oil
1 clove garlic
Salt and freshly ground black pepper

It's always best to use a big pan for pasta; it should have room to swell. Pour 2.25 litres (4 pt) water into the pan and add the olive oil. The oil prevents the pasta from sticking together. Peel the garlic and put the whole clove in the pan; bring the water to the boil. Add the tagliatelli and bring the water back to the boil again. Turn down to simmer. Stir the pasta gently as it cooks to prevent it from sticking together. (Fresh pasta will need only 1½–3 minutes, dried will need about 7–10. Follow the instructions on the packets.)

When the pasta is cooked, strain it through a sieve. Put it in a warm serving dish and season it with salt and pepper immediately. If you want to keep the tagliatelli warm for a little while, add more olive oil, cover it and keep in a cool oven.

Blackberry and Apple Pie

SERVES 6

WORKING TIME: 35 minutes preparation and cooking time.

225 g/8 oz blackberries
1 large cooking apple
1½ tablespoons caster sugar
1 clove
Rich Sweetened Shortcrust Pastry (see Cherry Tart, page 74)
1 teaspoon grated lemon rind

Wash the blackberries and peel, core and quarter the apple. Put the fruit and the remaining ingredients into a pan without any water. Heat through until the juices have been drawn. Set to one side to cool.

Roll out half the pastry about 5 mm (¼ in) thick. Let it stand for 10 minutes before covering the bottom of the pie dish with it. (The pastry stretches when it is rolled and leaving it for some minutes gives it a chance to settle.)

Put the fruit into the pie, heaping it up a little towards the centre. Roll out the rest of the pastry and cover the pie.

Bake in a preheated 220°C/425°F/Gas mark 7 oven for 5 minutes and then turn the oven down to a moderate 180°C/350°F/Gas mark 4 for about 15 minutes.

Serve hot or cold – I prefer cold.

IT was while I was at Stratford that Herbert Wise asked me to play Tiberius in *I Claudius* – a very happy job, due greatly to the wonderful adaptation by Jack Pulman.

I did some research into my part, and didn't altogether like what I found. Historically Claudius was a monster, a libertine and, once he had settled on Capri, a sexual fiend. But he also had strengths. He was a good soldier and a wonderful administrator; very good at looking after the roads. He doesn't come down to us as a fine Emperor. I think Robert Graves was very kind to him – perhaps sorry for him because he had that dreadful mother. Certainly I felt sorry for him. I think he must have been schizophrenic.

When a Capri fisherman bringing him a carp as a present startled him in his garden, Tiberius rubbed the man's skin off with the scales of the fish and threw them both over the cliff. Melons had to be served to him every day. His peacocks were more important to him than his soldiers. When one of his guards accidentally shot a peacock, he was executed.

All the Caesars seem to have exulted in gastronomic monomania. Tiberius paid a small fortune to an author who wrote a dialogue between mushrooms, fig-peckers, oysters and thrushes. His great fondness for mushrooms eventually led to his death from mushroom poisoning. He loved to eat partridge, for which he developed a fondness during his exile on Rhodes. The Greeks bred the birds for fighting; they are very warlike and fight to the death. But a selection went straight from the breeding pens to the 'Table Tiberius' and were spared a gladiatorial end.

MENU 2

GRILLED SARDINES

PARTRIDGE WITH TURNIPS

GREEN PEAS WITH CUCUMBER

MUSCATEL-GRAPE ICE

Grilled Sardines

SERVES 6

WORKING TIME: 15 minutes preparation and cooking time.

12–18 sardines (allow 2–3 per person)
2 tablespoons olive oil
Juice of 1 lemon
Salt and freshly ground black pepper
3 lemons
1 tablespoon chopped parsley

Ask your fishmonger to clean and gut the fish for you. Wash and dry them just before using.

Make 3 small incisions on each side of the fish, and brush them with olive oil. Season with the lemon juice, salt and pepper to taste.

Place the fish under a preheated grill, allowing about 4 minutes on each side. Divide the fish among 6 plates, cut the lemons in quarters, put 2 quarters on each plate, and sprinkle with chopped parsley. Serve.

Partridge with Turnips

SERVES 6

WORKING TIME: 1 hour preparation and cooking time.

3 turnips
2 teaspoons olive oil
2 partridges
1 glass of red wine
1 bay leaf
Salt and freshly ground black pepper
150 g/5 oz butter
3 eggs
1 tablespoon flour
Breadcrumbs
4 teaspoons Meat Glaze (see page 137)
1 teaspoon tarragon vinegar
150 ml/¼ pt double cream

Wash, peel and slice the turnips. Put them in a pan with sufficient water to cover and add the olive oil. Cook them until soft, drain, and keep warm.

Take all the flesh off the birds. Do this carefully so that you have nicely-shaped pieces of meat. Put the skin, the carcass and the bones in a pan. Pour in the red wine and add water to it so that the carcasses are covered. Add the bay leaf and season with salt and pepper to taste. Bring to the boil, and cook on a low heat to reduce the stock.

Melt the butter in a sauté pan and fry the partridge pieces until they turn golden brown.

Beat two of the eggs. Mix together a little flour, salt and pepper, then roll the fried pieces in it and dip them into the beaten egg. Toss the pieces in breadcrumbs and put them on a baking dish and into a preheated 220°C/425°F/Gas mark 7 oven for 15 minutes or until browned.

Strain the reduced stock from the carcasses of the partridge. Reserve 600 ml (1 pt) stock for use now. (Keep the rest to make game stock later, if liked.) Drain the fat from the sauté pan in which the partridge was fried and pour in the stock. And the Meat Glaze and the tarragon vinegar, and season with salt and pepper. Bring the stock to the boil, and cook until it has reduced by about one third.

Mash the turnips in a warm pan or bowl and add some butter, an egg and the cream. Season with salt and plenty of pepper. Put a spoonful of the mashed turnip under each slice of partridge, arranged equally among 6 plates, pour the sauce over and serve.

Green Peas with Cucumber

SERVES 6

WORKING TIME: 45 minutes preparation and cooking time.

900 g/2 lb unshelled garden peas or 350 g/12 oz frozen peas
500 g/18 oz cucumber
Salt and freshly ground black pepper
150 ml/¼ pt Vegetable Stock (see page 128)
2 tablespoons finely chopped fresh mint

If you are using garden peas, shell them. Then parboil for 3 or 4 minutes. Drain the peas and reserve. (If using frozen peas, just thaw. They don't need parboiling.)

Slice the cucumbers in half lengthways and remove the seeds. Slice the cucumber across into chunky slices.

Bring a saucepan of water to the boil and add the cucumbers. Cook for 2 minutes after the water has come to the boil again. Drain the cucumbers and reserve.

Bring the Vegetable Stock to the boil in a saucepan. Turn down the heat so that the stock is simmering, then add the peas and the cucumbers. Simmer for about 5 minutes.

Add the chopped mint and season with salt and pepper.

Muscatel-Grape Ice

SERVES 6

WORKING TIME: 30 minutes preparation time.

500 g/1 lb muscatel grapes
150 ml/¼ pt syrup (see Peppermint Ice Cream, page 45)
1 lemon
600 ml/1 pt double cream
1 glass Muscat de Beaumes de Venise

Put the grapes into a fine sieve and rub them through it into a bowl.

Add the syrup and the juice of the lemon. Place the grape mixture into the freezer.

In another bowl, whip the cream and add the Beaumes de Venise to it. Fold the chilled grape mixture and the whipped cream together and freeze until ready to serve.

TRIPE is really a dish of northern climes, whose delicate flavour and rib-binding hardiness is less appreciated in the south. I love all forms of tripe. Unfortunately, Sally and the girls don't like it much. It's the texture that worries them – as it does so many people.

I had taken a cottage for Christmas in Ilmington and had gone down some time before the holiday to finish a play I was writing for the B.B.C. I felt this was the moment to cook myself some tripe.

The next day I went down to the pub at lunch time, leaving the tripe ready to return to after my drink. The landlord, my friend Robin Shepherd, who has helped so much with this book, asked me if I wanted some lunch. 'Tripe,' I said. 'I've cooked myself some tripe.' This caused an immediate stir in the bar. It appeared that at least twenty men of the village were starved of tripe. There was only one thing for it, we had to have a tripe party and a date was set for when Sally was down from London.

The party was made up of disparate souls having one thing in common; tripe. It's amazing what food and wine will do to wave away suspicion, soften the temper and loosen the tongue.

MENU 3

THREE-FISH TERRINE

TRIPE AND ONIONS

MASHED POTATOES

(page 14)

WATERCRESS AND GREEN PEPPER SALAD

APPLES À LA PORTUGAISE

Three-Fish Terrine

SERVES 6

WORKING TIME: 25 minutes preparation and cooking time. Overnight to set.

225 g/8 oz white fish
100 g/4 oz smoked haddock
150 g/5 oz fresh salmon
1 glass dry white wine
3 tablespoons oil
Lemon juice
Salt and freshly ground black pepper
1 egg
1 teaspoon Dijon mustard
1 tablespoon double cream
1 teaspoon chopped green fennel leaves

Remove the skin from the white fish and the haddock. (It's easier to remove the skin from the salmon after it has been cooked.)

Cook each fish in a separate saucepan with a little of the white wine, a tablespoon of oil and the lemon juice to taste. Remove the fish from their respective saucepans and mash the flesh in three separate bowls. Reserve the cooking waters in one of the saucepans. Season each fish with salt and pepper.

Separate the egg; beat the white and reserve the yolk.

Stir the Dijon mustard into the reserved fish stock and boil until the liquid has reduced a little. Then stir in the cream and the beaten egg yolk. Add the chopped fennel.

Fold a little of the beaten egg white into each fish paste, then combine the white fish with a third of the creamy fennel sauce. Spread it across the bottom of a small terrine dish. Mix the salmon with a third of the sauce and make that the middle layer. Finally, fold the last third of the sauce into the haddock and make it your top layer.

Pour 600–750 ml (1–1½ pt) water into a baking tin. Stand the uncovered terrine in it and bake for 25 minutes in a preheated moderate 180°C/350°F/Gas mark 4 oven. Cover the terrine with greaseproof paper, weight it and leave it to set overnight. Before serving, turn out and cut it into slices.

Tripe and Onions

SERVES 6

THERE are several different sorts of tripe. The most usual are the honeycomb, the sponge, and the black. For this recipe use either the sponge or the honeycomb.

WORKING TIME: 3 hours or more soaking time. 35 minutes cooking time.

675 g/1½ lb tripe
600 ml/1 pt milk
1 clove garlic
1 bay leaf
Salt and freshly ground black pepper
4 medium onions
2 glasses dry white wine
1 teaspoon Dijon mustard
1 tablepoon lemon juice
2 tablespoons butter
1 tablespoon flour

Cut the tripe into strips and then into pieces. Soak it in the milk with a clove of garlic, bay leaf, salt and pepper for at least 3 hours.

Drain the tripe and reserve the liquid.

Peel and slice the onions. In a saucepan, simmer the tripe with the onions, dry white wine, Dijon mustard and the lemon juice, until the onions are soft and the tripe cooked. Slowly add the reserved liquid to the sauce. Roll the butter and the flour into balls and thicken the sauce, stirring over the heat. Add more pepper and salt, if necessary, and serve.

Watercress and Green Pepper Salad

SERVES 6

WORKING TIME: 25 minutes preparation time.

3 green peppers
350 g/12 oz watercress
1 tablespoon walnut or virgin olive oil
2 tablespoons lemon juice
Salt and freshly ground black pepper

Cut the tops off the peppers. Remove the seeds and ribs, and slice the peppers into thin strips. Put them in a bowl.

Remove the stalks from the watercress. Add the leaves to the peppers, pour the oil over, and toss. Sprinkle over the lemon juice and salt and pepper to taste. (Don't add too much pepper as the salad needs to retain a sharp, tangy taste.)

Apples à la Portugaise

SERVES 6

WORKING TIME: 40 minutes preparation and cooking time.

6 medium cooking apples
Lemon juice
12 cloves
300 ml/½ pt syrup (see Peppermint Ice Cream, page 45)
Apricot jam
Glacé cherries

Peel and core the apples and rub them with lemon juice. Stick 2 cloves in each apple. Put the apples in a saucepan with the syrup and cover with a lid. Cook slowly until the apples are tender but still firm.

Take out the apples and remove the cloves. Fill the centres with apricot jam and put a cherry on top of each. Serve with the syrup.

IMMEDIATELY after finishing *I, Claudius*, I was asked to go to New Zealand to play Inspector Alleyn in a quartet of Ngaio Marsh books which had been adapted for television. Each film was set in a different part of the Islands. I saw the country from the Bay of Islands in the north to Invercargill in the south.

Horses and self-catering dominated my five months there. I was taken to the trotting races on my second night in Auckland and introduced to the President of the Trotting Association. John Sullivan, his wife Aynsley, and their family of ten became a second home for me. They had a cottage in the grounds of their house which they lent me as a base when I was rehearsing in Auckland.

Aynsley is the first woman to hold a trainer's certificate in N.Z. All the children rode and, when Sally and Sarah were flown over to join me through the kindness of South Pacific Television, Sarah learnt to ride on a quite old pony called Blaze. Now, fourteen years later, my two-year-old granddaughter, Rosie, has had a walk round the field on Blaze, twenty-eight years old and not out!

I was passed from horse to horse, one introduction leading to another. I rode over many sheep stations and up and down a great many hills. We drove from location to location and I took my kitchen essentials in the boot of the car. We stayed at self-catering hotels, and ate a lot of lamb and a lot of fish.

Fennel grows in abundance in the hedgerows there but is regarded as a noxious weed. I picked it by the handful to flavour my fish and my salads.

MENU 4

APOSTLES IN THEIR COFFINS

BAKED RED MULLET WITH FENNEL

SAUTÉ POTATOES

CREAMED SPINACH

BLACKCURRANT FOOL

Apostles in their Coffins

SERVES 6

WORKING TIME: 10 minutes preparation time.

2 medium cucumbers
2 tins sardines in oil
3 tomatoes
1 tablespoon chopped basil
Salt and freshly ground black pepper
Lemon juice
1 head of lettuce

Cut the cucumbers into pieces the approximate size of a sardine. Hollow out the centres. Into each cucumber 'coffin' place a sardine.

Thinly slice the tomatoes and lay them on the fish so that the 'body' is covered. Sprinkle with chopped basil and season with lemon juice, salt and pepper to taste.

Chop the lettuce so as to make a bed for the coffins.

Baked Red Mullet with Fennel

SERVES 6

WORKING TIME: 35 minutes preparation and cooking time.

6 red mullet
2 tablespoons sunflower oil
2 medium onions
1 bulb fennel
1 tablespoon lemon juice
600 ml/1 pt Fish or Vegetable Stock (see page 128)
Flour and butter for thickening
Salt and freshly ground black pepper

Ask your fishmonger to clean and gut the fish. Wash them and make 3 incisions on either side of each fish. Rub with a little oil.

Peel and cut the onion. Finely chop it in a food processor or blender. Wash the fennel bulb and cut up as much as you can without using the stalk.

Soften the onion and the fennel in a pan with some oil.

Lightly oil an ovenproof and flameproof dish. Spread the softened vegetables on the bottom and lay the fish on them. Bake in a preheated 200°C/400°F/Gas mark 6 oven for 25 minutes. Transfer the fish to a serving platter and keep warm. Over a good heat stir the lemon juice and stock into the onion and fennel. Allow to reduce slightly, then thicken with a little flour and butter made into balls. Season to taste with salt and pepper. Serve the fennel beside the fish.

Sauté Potatoes

SERVES 6

WORKING TIME: 30 minutes preparation and cooking time.

800 g/1¾ lb potatoes
Salt and freshly ground black pepper
60 g/2½ oz butter

Peel and slice the potatoes. Dry them and season with salt and pepper.

In a large frying pan fry the sliced potatoes for about 25 minutes in butter, tossing and stirring gently.

An alternative preparation for sauté potatoes parboils them in their skin until they are nearly done. Allow them to cool and then peel them. Cut them into slices and fry for about 15 minutes in 60 g (2½ oz) butter.

Creamed Spinach

SERVES 6

WORKING TIME: 15 minutes preparation and cooking time.

1.5 kg/3 lb spinach
Salt and freshly ground black pepper
2 tablespoons butter
2 tablespoons double cream

Cut away the stalk and the hard vein at the back of each spinach leaf. Put the spinach into a saucepan with about a tablespoon of water. Season with salt and pepper and cover. Cook the spinach over a medium flame for about 8 minutes.

Drain off all water by pressing the spinach. Put it through the blender or food processor. Melt the butter in a saucepan, stir in the spinach purée, then add the cream and season to taste. Heat through, stirring gently.

Blackcurrant Fool

SERVES 6

WORKING TIME: 30 minutes preparation and cooking time.

425 g/1 lb blackcurrants
1 tablespoon sweet sherry
100 g/4 oz caster sugar
300 ml/½ pt double cream

Wash the blackcurrants. There is no need to remove the stems. Put the fruit, 1 tablespoon water and the sherry into a saucepan. Cover with a lid and cook until the fruit is soft, about 10 minutes.

Rub the fruit and juices through a fine sieve into a saucepan. Mix in the sugar.

Whip the cream into stiff peaks, then fold the blackcurrant purée into it. Pour the fool into a serving dish and chill in the fridge for several hours before serving.

PRUNES with bacon, prunes with anchovies, prunes with pâté. It was always prunes I was after when I sat in the kitchen in Varna, Bulgaria, as a small boy. There is a way they have of doing them in the Balkans, crushed and in strips, like a chew bar. We always bought them at the Fair when it came to town at Easter.

Father took a long time over his breakfast. The sun shone over his shoulder, the smoke of his morning cigarette curled up the sun's rays. He was much older than my mother, twenty-four years older. He was in the autumn of his life and seemed in no hurry to get to the Fair.

His soul has in its Autumn, when his wings
He furleth close; contented so to look
On mists in idleness – to let fair things
Pass by unheeded as a threshold brook.

Human Seasons
KEATS

Poor man, having young children who couldn't wait to see the motorbike riders whizzing round the wall of death, who couldn't wait to be bought a stick of crushed prunes!

The other delight was the *booza* from the sellers with the mobile urns. *Booza* is a maize-based, brown, milky drink. It seemed innocuous but was definitely alcoholic. I wonder if the our word 'boozer' owes its origin to the Balkan drink?

MENU 5

PRUNES WITH DUCK LIVER PÂTÉ

RIS DE VEAU DAMIDOFF

BOILED ONIONS

SWEET-AND-SOUR MUSHROOMS

BANANAS AU RHUM

Prunes with Duck Liver Pâté

SERVES 6

THIS pâté can be served as a separate dish on its own. If you decide to do this, transfer the seasoned pâté from the blender to a pâté pot or 4 small ramekins. It will keep if you melt some butter over the top.

WORKING TIME: 12 hours soaking time for prunes. 40 minutes preparation and cooking time.

FOR THE PÂTÉ

3 ducks' livers
1 clove garlic
1 tablespoon cognac
Salt and freshly ground black pepper

FOR THE PRUNE CANAPES

12 large prunes
1 tablespoon double cream
2 small tins anchovy fillets
12 small circular pieces fried bread
1 tablespoon butter
Watercress

Wash the liver and trim away any discoloured bits. Peel the clove of garlic.

Bring the brandy and 1 tablespoon water to the boil and cook the liver in it for 2 minutes. Drain the liver and put it with the garlic into a blender or food processor, and blend until smooth. Season with salt and pepper. Reserve for the prune stuffing or use as pâté on its own.

Soak the prunes in water overnight.

Drain the prunes and cut each one with a cross. Carefully take out the stone, keeping the shape of the prune.

Press the liver pâté through a fine sieve into a bowl. Whip the cream and stir it into the pâté.

With a forcing bag fill the prunes with the purée. Wind the anchovy fillets round the prunes, almost to the top.

Fry the circular pieces of bread and drain off the fat onto kitchen paper. Put a little of the purée on each piece of bread and then put the stuffed prunes and anchovies on top. Garnish with watercress.

Ris de Veau Damidoff

SERVES 6

WORKING TIME: 1 hour soaking time. 45 minutes preparation and cooking time.

2 sweetbreads
1 carrot
1 onion
1 turnip
1 tablespoon butter
4 pieces of fat bacon
300 ml/½ pt Brown Stock (see page 126)
Madeira Sauce (see page 138)

Soak the sweetbreads for an hour. Drain thoroughly and put them on a plate. Place a small chopping board or another plate on top of them and weight down until they get cold. Remove the weight and trim off the sinew and the fat.

Slice the carrot, the onion and the turnip. Put them in a saucepan with a little butter, sweat the vegetables gently and add the stock, stirring.

Cut the rinds off the bacon. Put the sweetbreads on the vegetables, and arrange the bacon strips over the sweetbreads. Cover the saucepan with a well-fitting lid and braise gently for 30 minutes.

Remove the bacon from the sweetbreads and serve with Madeira Sauce.

Boiled Onions

SERVES 6

WORKING TIME: 35 minutes preparation and cooking time.

18 small onions
4 or 5 cloves
2 tablespoons butter
Salt and freshly ground black pepper

Bring 750 ml (1½ pt) water to the boil in a saucepan under a steamer. Peel the onions, stick the cloves in them and put them into the steamer. Cook the onions until they are soft, about 25 minutes.

Drain, remove the cloves and turn the onions into a warm serving dish. Top with the butter, season to taste and put them in a warm oven for a few minutes, then toss to coat and serve.

Sweet-and-Sour Mushrooms

SERVES 6

WORKING TIME: 15 minutes preparation and cooking time.

225 g/8 oz mushrooms
2 tablespoons malt vinegar
1 tablespoon sunflower oil
2 teaspoons caster sugar

Peel the mushrooms and put them in a large flat saucepan with all the other ingredients and 150 ml (¼ pt) water. Bring to the boil, then allow to simmer for a few minutes until the mushrooms are tender.

Bananas au Rhum

SERVES 6

WORKING TIME: 15 minutes preparation and cooking time.

6 bananas
1 tablespoon butter
2 tablespoons lemon juice
2 teaspoons sugar
2 tablespoons dark rum

Peel the bananas and slice them in half lengthways. Lay them on a sheet of aluminium foil and add the other ingredients. Wrap the foil around the bananas.

Bake for 10 minutes in a preheated 220°C/425°F/Gas mark 7 oven. Serve with some of the syrup that has collected in the foil.

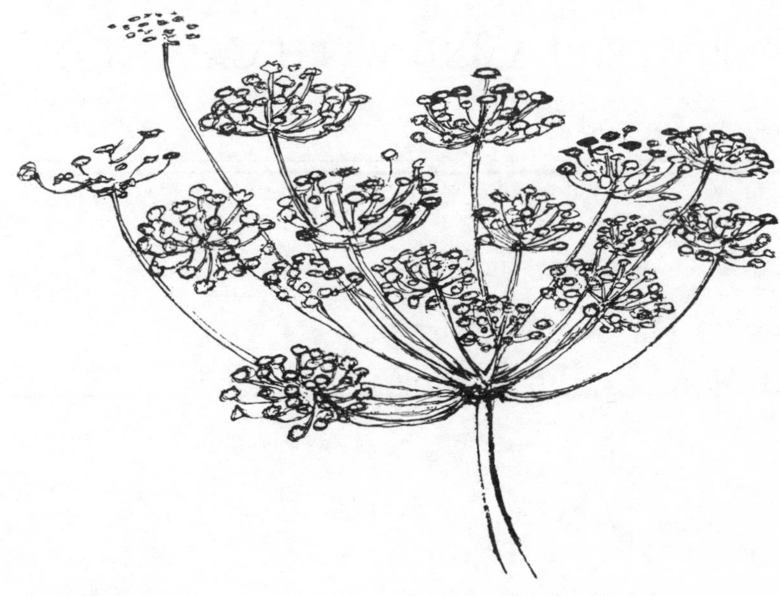

A change of tack in my career; the writing had taken hold and the commissions were coming in slowly but steadily. My first television play was produced by the B.B.C. with Charles Dance playing Siegfried Sassoon and David Sibley, Wilfred Owen. Charlie and David were wonderful and the play won an award of merit in the U.N.E.S.C.O. Peace Prize.

On to directing and writing training films and corporate videos. I was getting to the stage when I thought that I might give up acting altogether.

> The wine of life keeps oozing drop by drop,
> The leaves of life keep falling one by one.

Wrong! Another change in my career. I was offered the part of Inspector Wexford in the Ruth Rendell Mysteries. I thought I was in the autumn of life and find I'm in a second spring, though not so heady. Good steak and kidney pie time . . .

MENU 6

CHEESE ZEPHYRS

STEAK AND KIDNEY PIE IN ROUGH PUFF PASTRY

SPICED RED CABBAGE

APPLES FLAMED WITH CALVADOS

Cheese Zephyrs

SERVES 6

WORKING TIME: 30 minutes preparation and cooking time.

150 ml/¼ pt double cream
300 ml/½ pt milk
¾ tablespoon powdered gelatine
50 g/2 oz Parmesan cheese
Cayenne pepper
6 King prawns
1 tablespoon chopped parsley
6 slices lemon

Whip the cream and reserve.

Boil 150 ml (¼ pt) milk and dissolve the gelatine in it. Add the rest of the milk, the Parmesan cheese and season with cayenne pepper to taste. Simmer over a low heat, allowing it to reduce a little.

Remove the milk from the heat and carefully fold in the whipped cream. Pour the liquid into 6 ramekins and let them set.

Turn the zephyrs out, by warming the edges of the ramekins very slightly in hot water.

Peel the prawns, sprinkle the zephyrs with parsley and lay 1 King prawn on each one. Decorate with a slice of lemon.

Steak and Kidney Pie

SERVES 6

WORKING TIME: 2 hours preparation and cooking time.

800 g/1¾ lb beef steak
225 g/8 oz kidneys
1 tablespoon flour
Salt and freshly ground black pepper
1 onion
4 mushrooms
1 tablespoon red wine
½ teaspoon horseradish sauce
150 ml/¼ pt Brown Stock (see page 126)
½ quantity Rough Puff Pastry (see below)
1 egg yolk

Cut the steak into small pieces. Trim away most of the fat. Skin and trim the kidneys and cut into small pieces.

Mix the flour, salt and pepper to taste on a chopping board. Dip the pieces of steak and kidney into the seasoned flour, then put them in a pie dish. Fill the dish, heaping it towards the middle so that the crust will be raised.

Slice the onion and peel and slice the mushrooms. Pour the red wine into the dish and toss the wine and meat with the sliced onion, mushrooms and horseradish sauce. Use enough of the stock to fill the dish half full.

Wet the edge of the pie dish and put a border of pastry round it. Moisten it with a little water and put on the pastry lid. Trim and crimp the edges and score them with a pastry knife. Brush over lightly with the beaten egg yolk. Bake in a 220°C/425°F/Gas mark 7 oven for 1½ hours.

Rough Puff Pastry

WORKING TIME: 20 minutes preparation time. 30 minutes standing time, at least.

100 g/4 oz butter
50 g/2 oz lard
Pinch of salt
225 g/8 oz flour
½ teaspoon lemon juice
Ice cold water

The butter and lard should be as cold as possible. Sieve the flour and the salt into a clean dry bowl. Cut the butter and the lard into the flour and mix lightly and quickly together.

Make a well in the centre of the flour. Pour in the lemon juice. Have some very cold water ready in a jug. Pour in a little water at a time, mixing lightly with a pallet knife until you have a stiffish dough.

Turn on to a floured baking board and shape into a long strip. Roll with short quick strokes away from you. Lift the dough constantly while rolling and turning, flouring the board to prevent sticking.

When you have rolled it into a strip about 15–18 cm (6–7 in) wide, dredge it with a little flour and fold it in 3. Turn one edge away from you towards the centre, then bring the furthest edge from you to cover both layers, meeting at the fold of the pastry. Press the edges down with a rolling pin. Half turn the pastry and roll out again. Repeat this process 3 times. Fold the pastry and let it stand in a cold place for 30 minutes before use. (You can wrap it in a piece of greaseproof paper and even keep it in a fridge for a day or two.)

Spiced Red Cabbage

SERVES 6

TRADITIONALLY Lancashire hot-pot is served with pickled red cabbage. This is a German recipe for *Roth Kraut* and goes very well indeed with the hot-pot.

WORKING TIME: 40 minutes preparation time. 45 minutes cooking time.

1 good-sized red cabbage
Caraway seeds
Salt and freshly ground black pepper
2 tablespoons butter or oil
2 tablespoons Vegetable Stock (see page 128) or water
½ glass white wine
¼ glass vinegar
2 teaspoons of sugar

Wash the cabbage, quarter it and cut out the stalks. Slice the cabbage. Sprinkle a few caraway seeds and some salt among the cabbage shreds, put it in a bowl and let it stand for 30 minutes.

Heat the butter in a pan and add the cabbage and the stock or water. Allow to simmer for 10 minutes. Add the wine and the vinegar, then put in the sugar.

Put a good close lid on the saucepan. If it doesn't fit tightly put a piece of greaseproof or aluminium foil over the pan and then cover with the lid. Cook over a low heat for another 35 minutes.

Apples Flamed with Calvados

SERVES 6

WORKING TIME: 20 minutes preparation and cooking time.

6 eating apples
50 g/2 oz butter
1 tablespoon caster sugar
½ glass dry cider
Calvados

Peel and core the apples. Arrange in an oven proof dish. Put a piece of butter and some sugar into each apple then pour the cider over them.

Cook in a preheated oven, 220°C/425°F/Gas mark 7, until they are just tender. Take them out of the oven and, if necessary, transfer to a flameproof dish. Keep them warm over a good heat.

Warm some Calvados in a small saucepan. Pour this over the apples and set them alight. Serve while still flaming.

INSPECTOR Wexford and I have much in common. We both love literature, etymology, humour and people. We both suffer the disadvantage of putting on weight. Ruth Rendell is quite specific about the old boy having to go on diets. I hate it as much as he does and have to do it as frequently. In fact, it seems that whenever *he* gets too fat *I* have to diet!

He and I went over to Honfleur to film some of 'A Sleeping Life'. We hugely enjoyed the Normandy lobsters, oysters, sea urchins and crab, the Langue de Boeuf and the Tripes à la Mode de Caen. I think we both agree that:

The day becomes more solemn and serene
When noon is past – there is a harmony
In Autumn and a lustre in its sky . . .

MENU 7

COCK-A-LEEKIE SOUP

GROUSE WITH BROWNED BREADCRUMBS AND WATERCRESS

BRUSSELS SPROUTS

BREAD SAUCE

(page 140)

POTATO CRISPS

ATHOL BROSE

Cock-a-Leekie Soup

SERVES 6 GENEROUSLY

YOU can make this soup two or three days before as it improves enormously by being reheated.

WORKING TIME: 2 hours 20 minutes preparation and cooking time.

8 medium leeks
1 chicken, weighing about 1½ kg/3 lb
50 g/2 oz butter
3 litres/5 pt Clear Stock (see page 129)
Salt and freshly ground black pepper
Lemon juice

Wash and trim the leeks. Bring some water to the boil in a saucepan and scald the leeks in it for 5 or 6 minutes.

Wash the fowl and cut it into small joints. Melt the butter in a saucepan and brown the pieces of fowl in it. Drain off the butter and add the stock. Bring to the boil. You will need to skim the soup at this stage.

Add 300 ml (½ pt) water, salt, pepper and lemon juice. Cut the leeks into slices and add them to the soup. Simmer for 2 hours. Look at the soup every now and again and remove the scum as it rises.

Take out the fowl and remove the meat from the bones. Cut the meat into pieces and put them into a tureen. Pour the leeks and broth over them.

Grouse with Browned Breadcrumbs and Watercress

SERVES 6

WITH this method of presentation, there should be no need for gravy. Breadcrumbs are traditionally served with grouse, and can be made with any stale leftover bread. Keep the dried breadcrumbs in an airtight tin and warm them when needed.

WORKING TIME: 45 minutes preparation and cooking time.

2 or 3 grouse, according to size (including liver and giblets)
50 g/2 oz butter
Lemon juice
Salt and freshly ground black pepper
3 or 4 pieces of bacon
6 slices of bread
A little flour
Several slices of stale bread
Watercress

Wash the birds inside and out, then dry them with a cloth.

Mix the butter and lemon juice to taste with some salt and pepper. Put a little of the seasoned butter inside each bird. Cover the breasts with bacon. Wrap each bird in greaseproof paper and then aluminium foil.

Lay the grouse on their breasts on a rack in a baking tin. Cook them in a preheated 200°C/400°F/Gas mark 6 oven for 25 to 35 minutes.

Melt a little butter in a frying pan and fry the livers in it for about 3 minutes. Mash them, add salt and pepper and reserve. Cut the crusts off the bread slices and fry them to a golden brown. Keep warm.

Unwrap the grouse, baste well, remove the bacon from the breasts and dredge them with a little flour. Return them, unwrapped, to the oven and let the breasts brown for 10–15 minutes.

To make breadcrumbs, place the stale bread on a baking tin in the bottom of the oven. When it is good and brown (about 10 minutes), put it in a processor or blender to process. (The breadcrumbs can be made ahead to this point and kept for several weeks in an airtight tin.) Return the fine crumbs to the baking tin with a little butter. Warm until the butter is melted, and toss the warm breadcrumbs in it.

To serve, spread the liver paste on the fried bread. Put the grouse on a serving dish, pour the pan fat over them, place the fried bread all round them, garnish with watercress and serve accompanied by a dish of breadcrumbs.

Brussels Sprouts

SERVES 6

WORKING TIME: 20 minutes preparation and cooking time.

800 g/1¾ lb sprouts
2 tablespoons butter
Salt and freshly ground black pepper
Nutmeg

Wash the sprouts and remove some of the outer leaves. Trim the stem and cut a cross on the bottom of the sprout.

Bring 900 ml (1½ pt) water to the boil in a saucepan under a steamer. When you have a good head of steam put in the sprouts. Cover and steam for 10 minutes or until the sprouts are tender.

Transfer the sprouts to a serving dish, toss them in the butter and season with salt, pepper and nutmeg.

Potato Crisps

SERVES 6 GENEROUSLY

WORKING TIME: 25 minutes preparation and cooking time.

4 medium firm potatoes (all roughly the same size)
1 litre/1¾ pt sunflower oil (depending on size of pan)
Salt

Wash and peel the potatoes. Slice them very thinly by hand or using a food processor. Put them in a bowl of cold water and leave to soak for about twelve minutes.

Heat the oil in your pan until it is very hot, about 185°C/365°F. Plunge the crisps at once into the fat. Drain on kitchen paper and sprinkle with salt.

When you are sure they have entirely been drained of fat, keep them in a warm oven until serving time.

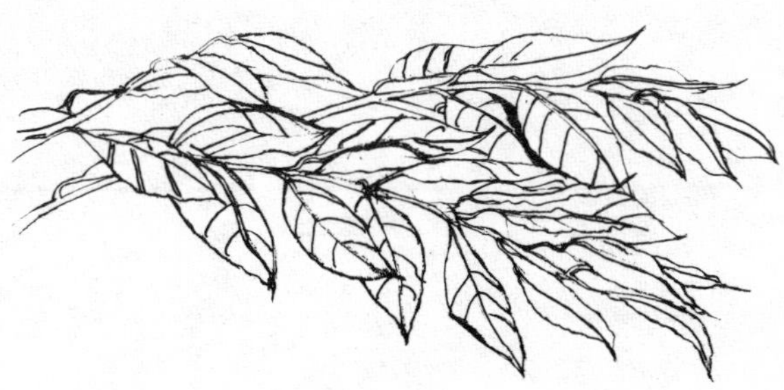

Athol Brose

SERVES 6

WORKING TIME: 45 minutes preparation and cooking time.

25 g/1 oz medium oatmeal
600 ml/1 pt double cream
3 tablespoons honey
3 tablespoons malt whisky

Put the oatmeal in a large dry frying pan and toast it until it is golden brown. Toss it frequently. Take the oatmeal out of the pan and let stand and cool.

Whip the cream until it is stiff and add the honey. Whip again and add the whisky. (You can add more honey or more whisky to taste.) Whip again.

Fold the toasted oatmeal into the cream and divide it between 6 wine glasses. Keep cool until ready to serve.

Stocks, Sauces and Other Basics

A good stock is the basis for all soups and gravies and a great many sauces. To turn a stock into a sauce there is usually a need for a thickening agent, a liaison. So I think it practical to deal with stocks, liaisons and sauces in that order.

STOCKS

THE basic stocks are a brown stock, a white stock, a fish stock and a vegetable stock. You can, of course, buy stock cubes which simplify your life but don't taste as good. Anyway, I enjoy having a stock pot doing its own thing on the stove.

The first principle is not to throw anything away; the bones of any joint of meat, the carcass of fowl, the peelings of vegetables or the water that the vegetables were cooked in all do service in a stock. You can buy bones from the butcher – he's only too glad to sell them to you quite cheaply. In the eighteenth century the knuckle end of a good marrow bone was often wrapped in a napkin and served as a first course.

There was a tradition in the Cork Opera House that during the interval any member of the public who felt he had talent could get up on stage and air it. On one particular evening a fiddler was scraping on his violin while a drunk was causing a disturbance in the gallery. There were raucous calls for the drunk to be thrown out. But out of the body of the audience the voice of reason sang out clear. 'Ah, no, don't waste him, throw him at the fiddler!'

I feel very much the same about a stock pot. Waste nothing; throw everything at it. The Scots sauce chef I worked with at the Regent Palace summed it up beautifully. 'Wi' a guid, carrefuully preparred broth there's no sauce ye canna make.'

Brown Stock

MAKES ABOUT 1.15 LITRES/2 PT

WORKING TIME: 35 minutes preparation time, 4 or 5 hours cooking time, at least.

1.5 kg/3 lb shin of beef with bone
900 g/2 lb lean beef
1.5 kg/3 lb knuckle of veal
2 tablespoons oil
2 onions
2 medium carrots
1 stalk celery
2 cloves
Bouquet garni of parsley, thyme, bay leaves
Salt and freshly ground black pepper

Ask your butcher to saw the shin of beef and its bone into chunks.

Cut the beef into good-sized pieces. Put the beef, the bones and the knuckle of veal into a baking pan with a tablespoon of oil and put it into a hot oven for 10 minutes.

Peel and chop the onions, the carrots and the celery. Add the vegetables and the rest of the oil to the pan. Turn down the heat and roast them for 10 minutes. Pour in a cup of water and continue to cook until the water has almost boiled away. Add another cup of water and allow that to reduce also. The stock should now be a good brown colour.

Transfer the stock to a saucepan and add the cloves, the bouquet garni and a little salt and pepper. (Not too much salt and pepper because the seasoning will come when making your required sauce.) Add enough water to cover the ingredients generously. Simmer for at least 4 hours, uncovered, and skim from time to time.

Strain through a sieve or muslin cloth, then reduce the stock to the consistency you like.

Ham Bone Stock

MAKES ABOUT 1.4 LITRES/2½ PT

WORKING TIME: 15 minutes preparation time. 3 hours cooking time.

2 unsmoked bacon hocks
2 small onions
4 cloves
2 carrots
6 peppercorns
¼ teaspoon nutmeg
Sprig of sage
Sprig of thyme
600 ml/1 pt dry cider

If you get green (or unsmoked) hocks there is really no need to soak them. Don't, however, add any salt. Put the hocks in a good heavy saucepan.

Peel the onions, stick the cloves into them and put them in the pot. Scrape and add the carrots, peppercorns, nutmeg and the herbs. Pour over the cider and add sufficient water to cover.

Bring to the boil, turn down the heat and let the stock simmer for 3 hours.

Take out the hocks and strain the liquid into a bowl through a scalded teacloth or a fine sieve.

Allow to cool overnight and then remove the fat with a large spoon. Cut the skin and fat off the hocks in one piece. If you have a garden, string the fat to a tree or a fence for the birds. They're very grateful for it in the winter.

Take the meat off the bones, cut it into cubes and serve it with a white parsley sauce. Cover the stock and keep it refrigerated, boiling up once or twice a week, until needed.

White Stock

MAKES ABOUT 1.4 LITRES/2½ PT

THIS stock can be made into a more chickeny-flavoured version by substituting chicken meat for the veal.

WORKING TIME: 35 minutes preparation time. 4 to 5 hours cooking time.

900 g/2 lb veal knuckle
900 g/2 lb veal pieces
900 g/2 lb chicken bones and giblets (or a chicken carcass)
3 medium onions
2 medium carrots
2 leeks
1 stalk celery
½ lemon
Bouquet garni of parsley, thyme, bay leaves
Salt and freshly ground black pepper

Put the bones and the meat pieces into a saucepan with sufficient water to cover and bring to the boil. Peel the onions and the carrots and slice in half. Wash the leeks and celery thoroughly.

Once the stock is boiling, turn down the heat and add the vegetables, the lemon, the herbs and a little salt and pepper. Simmer for at least 4 hours, uncovered, and skim from time to time.

Strain through a sieve or muslin cloth, return to the pan and reduce the stock to the consistency you require.

Fish Stock

MAKES ABOUT 1.4 LITRES/2½ PT

YOUR fishmonger will be only too delighted to supply you with haddock skin and bones and fish heads.

WORKING TIME: 30 minutes preparation time. 1½ hours cooking time.

1 cod's head
Some haddock skin and bones
2 onions
½ bulb fennel
Bouquet garni of sweet basil, thyme, chervil
1 glass white wine
Pepper

Put the fish head and haddock skin and bone into a saucepan with sufficient water to cover. Bring to the boil and skim off any scum.

Peel the onions and slice them. Wash the fennel bulb and, if necessary, cut away the outside leaves. Slice the bulb and tie the herbs into a muslin bag. Turn down the heat and add the vegetables, the bouquet garni, white wine and pepper. Allow to simmer for 1½ hours.

Strain through a sieve or muslin cloth and reserve until needed.

Vegetable Stock

MAKES ABOUT 1.15 LITRES/2 PT

THIS stock can be used for all vegetarian sauces and all vegetable soups. If you have enough, you can use this stock instead of water for your basic brown stock (see page 127).

WORKING TIME: 45 minutes preparation and cooking time.

2 leeks
2 onions
1 potato
2 stalks celery
Bouquet garni (of any herbs you like)
Salt and freshly ground black pepper
Peelings or stalks from the vegetables you might be using – cauliflower leaves, cabbage stalks, potato peelings, etc.
Vegetable water from either steamed or boiled vegetables

Wash the leeks and slice them, using as much leek as you can. Peel and slice the onions, wash and quarter the potato, and trim the celery. Add any vegetables or outer leaves you want to use up.

Put all the ingredients into a saucepan; cover with enough vegetable water to cover. Add salt and pepper to taste. Bring the stock to the boil and then allow to simmer very gently for 30 minutes. Strain through a sieve.

Clear Stock or Consommé

SERVES 6

WORKING TIME: 15 minutes preparation time. 30 minutes cooking time.

1.4 litres/2½ pt Brown Stock (see page 126)
100 g/4 oz lean beef
½ turnip
1 carrot
1 stalk celery
6 or 7 peppercorns
1 onion
2 cloves
1 sprig parsley
¼ teaspoon mace or fenugreek
Whites and shells of 2 eggs

Take 1.4 litres (2½ pt) of good stock, making sure that no traces of fat remain. Put the stock into a saucepan.

Take any fat off the meat and put the meat through the mincer. Wash, peel and slice all the vegetables. Put the meat, the vegetables and the herbs and spices into the saucepan. Whisk the whites of the eggs and add them to the pan. You need to wash the shells very well before you crush them and also add them to the pan. Whisk the soup as it comes to boiling. Remove the whisk and let the soup boil for a moment. Lower the heat and let it simmer for 20 minutes.

Strain the broth through a cloth. If it isn't quite clear the first time, strain it again. When the soup is clear add water, or a mixture of water and white wine, to bring it to the consistency you require.

Consommé à la Royale

SERVES 6

ONCE you have clarified or clear soup (above) you have consommé. The consommé then takes its name from what you put into it.

WORKING TIME: 5 minutes preparation time. 10 to 15 minutes cooking time.

1.15 litres/2 pt clear soup (see above)

FOR THE CUSTARD
3 eggs
150 ml/¼ pt White Stock (see page 127)
¼ teaspoon fenugreek
Salt and freshly ground black pepper

Use as a base the clear soup or consommé from the preceding recipe, adding a mixture of water and wine to bring it to the consistency you require.

To make the savoury custard, grease the inside of a small pudding basin, beat 2 yolks and 1 whole egg and put them into the basin. Add the stock and the salt, pepper and fenugreek. Put the basin into a steamer or into a saucepan of hot water. Cook it very gently until the custard becomes firm. Let it cool. Turn it out on to a board and cut it into fancy shapes.

Heat up the consommé. Put the custard shapes into a serving bowl and pour the boiling consommé over them.

ROUX AND LIAISONS

ALL sauces must have something to bind them or thicken them. It is called a liaison – and if it includes an egg it can be tricky, because it can curdle.

Liaisons can be made with butter and cream, with eggs, with butter and wheatflour flour – mixed at the time as when making a Sauce Blanche – or with potato flour, cornflour, pearl barley or rice.

The most basic liaison is a roux, made simply with butter or flour. You can have brown roux, white roux or blond roux. The nice thing about roux is that you can make it sometime in advance and keep it until it is needed. You simply put it in a covered jar and put it in the fridge.

Here are some basic rules of thumb:

One tablespoon of roux will thicken 2 cups of liquid.

Put the roux into a pan and stir in the stock to be thickened gradually, stirring all the time.

Stir until boiling and the stock thickens.

Brown Roux

WORKING TIME: 15 minutes cooking time.

225 g/8 oz butter **225 g/8 oz flour**

Melt the butter over a low heat, slowly add the flour, blend and cook gently until it changes colour and becomes brown.

Put it into a jar and keep it for use.

White and Blond Roux

WORKING TIME: 15 minutes cooking time.

225 g/8 oz butter **225 g/8 oz flour**

For a white roux, melt the butter over a low heat. Add the flour, stirring all the time, until it becomes a firm paste. You must make sure that it does not begin to colour. Cook it for 15 minutes.

Put in a jar and keep it for use.

For a blond roux, do everything exactly the same as for the brown and white roux, but take it off the heat as soon as it begins to colour slightly.

Again, you can store it in a jar for when you want to use it.

Potato Flour or Cornflour Thickening

WORKING TIME: 15 minutes cooking time.

Blend the potato flour or the cornflour with a little cold water, stock or milk in a bowl. The sauce must be boiling when you stir in the liaison.

Once it is blended, simmer for 10 to 15 minutes.

Butter and Cream Liaison

WORKING TIME: 5–8 minutes cooking time.

To a hot sauce in a pan you add an equal proportion of butter and cream.

Cut the butter into small pieces. Drop a piece at a time into the sauce and whisk until all are absorbed. Do the same with a spoonful of cream.

Whisk it all the time and don't let it boil.

Butter and Flour Liaison

WORKING TIME: 5 minutes cooking time.

This is really quite simple. Knead some flour and butter together into small balls. Then drop them into the hot sauce one at a time, stirring until each one is absorbed before dropping in the next.

Egg Liaison

WORKING TIME: 5 minutes cooking time.

Beat up 1 or 2 egg yolks in a bowl with a little cream or milk. Add some of the hot stock or sauce to the liaison, gradually, and blend well. You can take the saucepan off the heat and stir in the liaison until the eggs thicken. Don't let the mixture boil or the eggs will curdle.

SAUCES

Melted Butter Sauce

MAKES ABOUT 600 ML/1 PT

WORKING TIME: 5 minutes cooking time.

75 g/3 oz butter
4 tablespoons flour
3 teaspoons Dijon mustard
300 ml/½ pt Vegetable Stock (see page 128) or water
1 glass dry white wine
1 tablespoon lemon juice

Melt the butter in a pan, add the flour and blend, making sure there are no lumps. Gradually stir in the stock or water. Add the white wine, the Dijon mustard and the lemon juice. Stir until boiling, then simmer for about 5 minutes. If the sauce is too runny continue to simmer until you reach the right consistency.

Sauce Bechamel

MAKES ABOUT 600 ML/1 PT

BECHAMEL sauce is probably the all-important sauce in cooking. It is the starting point of many main dishes and can be flavoured in a variety of ways to accompany fish, poultry or veal. Cheese can be added to it for gratin dishes and it can serve as the basis for some desserts.

If you have white roux in the fridge you can use that and stir the milk into it. Bechamel will keep in the fridge if boiled through every day or so.

WORKING TIME: 15 minutes cooking time.

4 tablespoons butter
50 g/2 oz flour
600 ml/1 pt milk
Salt and freshly ground black pepper

Heat the butter in a saucepan, stir in the flour and mix well with a wooden spoon. Add the milk, pouring steadily while stirring. Make sure that the sauce does not go lumpy. It will take fairly enthusiastic stirring.

When you have added all the milk your sauce is ready. Season it as you like.

Sauce Bearnaise

MAKES 300 ML/½ PT

THIS sauce is delicious with grilled fish, meat or poultry.

WORKING TIME: 25 minutes preparation and cooking time.

1 tablespoon chopped shallots
2 tablespoons chopped chervil and tarragon
½ bay leaf
3 tablespoons tarragon vinegar
Salt and freshly ground black pepper
2 egg yolks
100 g/4 oz butter
1 teaspoon lemon juice

Put the chopped shallots, half the chopped herbs and ½ bay leaf, and the vinegar with some salt and pepper to the pan. Reduce the liquid to one-third. Take it off the heat and allow it to cool slightly.

Mix the 2 egg yolks with 1 tablespoon water. Add the eggs to the pan and heat over a low flame, whisking all the time, until the eggs have thickened. Cut the butter into small pieces and drop them into the pan a piece at a time, whisking constantly.

When the consistency is smooth take the sauce off the heat. Add the second tablespoon of herbs, mix the lemon juice well in, and keep the sauce warm.

Sauce Bercy (Marrow Sauce)

MAKES ABOUT 300 ML/½ PT

TO make this sauce you will need to extract the marrow from some beef bones. You can either stand the chopped bones in cold water for an hour or so, or heat them in a gentle oven until the marrow softens and comes away quite easily. Sauce Bercy can be served with fish, grills, eggs, calves liver, and kidneys.

WORKING TIME: 45 minutes cooking and preparation.

3 good-sized marrow bones, cut up (they will produce about 150 g/6 oz marrow)
1 tablespoon chopped shallots
100 g/4 oz softened butter
1 bay leaf
A sprig of thyme
Salt and freshly ground black pepper
1 small glass dry white wine
300 ml/½ pt White Stock (see page 127)
Juice of ½ lemon
1 tablespoon chopped parsley

Blanch the marrow in a little salted water. Drain, reserving the water, and leave the marrow to cool. Peel and chop the shallots.

Sweat the chopped shallots in half the butter. Do not allow them to brown. Add the bay leaf, thyme, salt and pepper. Add 2 tablespoons of the marrow water and the white wine. Reduce until only half the liquid remains. Stir in the White Stock and reduce again. Pass the sauce through a sieve.

Return the sauce to a low heat. Slice the marrow and add it to the sauce. Stir in the remaining softened butter, the lemon juice and the chopped parsley. Transfer to a sauceboat.

Brown Sauce

MAKES 500 ML/17 FL OZ

THIS brown sauce is a simplification of Sauce Espagnole. If you make this basic sauce before you need it, you can boil it up every other day or so, and it will keep in the fridge for a week or ten days.

It can be used for gravies, braised dishes, brown stews. You can reduce it to make glazes.

WORKING TIME: 1 hour preparation and cooking time.

1 onion
2 tablespoons butter
25 g/1 oz flour
550 ml/18 fl oz Brown Stock (see page 126)
1 carrot
2 stalks celery
1 small turnip or parsnip
2 cloves
¼ teaspoon mace
7 peppercorns
Salt
Bouquet garni of sage, parsley, thyme and mint

Peel and slice the onion. Melt the butter in a saucepan, add the onion, and stir until it is brown. Add the flour and stir in. Take the saucepan off the heat and blend in the stock gradually, making sure that it is smooth.

Put the saucepan back on the heat and stir until boiling, about 5 minutes. You will then need to skim it.

Wash, peel and slice the other vegetables and add them to the sauce, together with the herbs and the seasonings. Simmer gently for 30 minutes.

Strain the sauce through a sieve or muslin cloth.

Sauce Espagnole

MAKES 1 LITRE/1¾ PT

THIS is the complicated and time-consuming version of a Brown Sauce, but it does taste very good. This sauce will keep for two weeks in a fridge. It should be boiled up occasionally.

WORKING TIME: 2 hours preparation and cooking time.

1 onion
½ celeriac root
2 shallots
1 carrot
4 tablespoons butter
150 g/5 oz veal pieces
150 g/5 oz ham
Chicken remains
Remains of any game (optional)
1 teaspoon tomato purée
Salt
4 cloves
8 peppercorns
Bay leaf
Pinch of mace
Pinch of nutmeg
Bouquet garni
3 litres/5 pt Brown Stock (see page 126)
1 glass claret
1 glass Madeira or sherry
4 or 5 sliced mushrooms
100 g/4 oz flour

Wash, peel and slice the vegetables. Melt 2 tablespoons butter in a saucepan, add the vegetables and brown them.

Cut the veal and ham into small pieces and add them along with any chicken or game meat to the saucepan. Stir in the tomato purée, seasoning and the herbs. Keep stirring until they too are a light brown.

Take the pan off the heat and pour off the fat. Now add the stock and the wines and the mushrooms. Bring the stock to the boil, turn down the heat and simmer for about an hour. Skim frequently. This skimming is very important in all stock making. If the scum is not skimmed off you will have no shine to the sauce.

Melt the remaining 2 tablespoons butter in a large saucepan, stir in the flour and brown it gently. Add the sauce gradually, stirring all the time. Allow to boil, then turn down the heat and simmer for 1 hour. Remember to stir every now and then. Skim and then strain it.

Sauce Créole

MAKES ABOUT 900 ML/1½ PT

WORKING TIME: 15 minutes preparation time. 20 minutes cooking time.

3 small onions
3 celery stalks
1 green pepper
1 clove garlic
2 tablespoons oil
1 tablespoon lemon juice
400 g/14 oz tin peeled tomatoes
1 tablespoon sugar
1 teaspoon cornflour
1 teaspoon paprika
½ teaspoon salt
1 tablespoon chopped basil

Chop the onions, the celery, the green pepper and the garlic finely and sauté in the oil and lemon juice. When they are soft, add the tomatoes and the sugar.

Mix the cornflour with 1 tablespoon water and add that to the pan.

Season with the paprika, salt and chopped basil. Bring the sauce to the boil, then allow to simmer in an uncovered pan for about 20 minutes, by which time it should have thickened and reduced. Stir occasionally.

Sauce Portugaise

MAKES 500 ML/¾ PT

THIS is a strong-flavoured, tomato sauce that compliments fish like cod, and shellfish, poultry and veal.

WORKING TIME: 40 minutes preparation and cooking time.

2 large onions
2 cloves garlic
1 tablespoon olive oil
4 tomatoes
150 ml/¼ pt White or Brown Stock (see pages 127 and 126)
2 tablespoons butter
1 tablespoon flour
1 tablespoon chopped parsley

Peel and finely chop the onions and the garlic. (Use a blender to do this, if you wish.) Place in a saucepan with the olive oil and cook until the onions are soft.

Peel and deseed the tomatoes. Mash them with a fork in a bowl. Add the mashed tomatoes to the onions and let them cook slowly for 25 minutes, or until the tomatoes are reduced to a pulp. Pour in the stock and cook for a further 10 minutes.

Thicken the sauce by kneading balls of butter and flour together and dropping them into the sauce, stirring all the time until the butter melts and the sauce thickens. Sprinkle the chopped parsley over the sauce.

Sauce Velouté

MAKES 600 ML/1 PT

THIS is really a Bechamel sauce, but the liquid added is stock not milk. It goes well with fish and fowl. The simple addition of parsley turns this into Parsley Sauce.

WORKING TIME: 20 minutes preparation and cooking time.

4 tablespoons butter
50 g/2 oz flour
2 tablespoons lemon juice
600 ml/1 pt White Stock (see page 127)
Salt and freshly ground black pepper
1 teaspoon Dijon mustard (optional)

Melt the butter in a saucepan. Add the flour and blend it in carefully. Don't let it colour in the cooking. Take the pan off the heat and mix in the stock gradually. Let it boil and then turn down the heat and simmer for a few minutes.

Add the lemon juice and season to taste. Mustard is not in the classic tradition, but if you are using the velouté as the basis for a Parsley Sauce then the mustard enriches it.

GLAZES

Meat Glaze

MAKES 900 ML/1½ PT

THIS glaze makes a good aspic-like coating for cold meats such as beef and veal roasts.

WORKING TIME: 1½ hours cooking time.

2.5 litres/4½ pt Brown Stock (see page 126)

Reduce the stock until it becomes sticky. When cold it makes a jelly or aspic.

Demi-Glaze

MAKES ABOUT 600 ML/1 PT

THIS demi-glaze is a more finely flavoured version of the meat glaze.

WORKING TIME: 1 hour cooking time.

600 ml/1 pt Espagnole or Brown Sauce (see pages 135 and 134)
900 ml/1½ pt Clear Stock (see page 129)

Put the ingredients into a saucepan and boil. Turn the heat down to simmer and reduce by two-thirds.

OTHER BASICS

Madeira Sauce

MAKES 900 ML/1½ PT

WORKING TIME: 25 minutes cooking time.

600 ml/1 pt Demi-Glaze (see page 137)
2 teaspoons Meat Glaze (see page 137)
1 glass Madeira

Heat the Demi-Glaze and add the Madeira. Boil for 15 minutes. Add the Meat Glaze, stirring, and heat gently. Use as desired.

Sauce Chaudfroid

MAKES ABOUT 550 ML/18 FL OZ

YOU can, of course, use packet aspic jelly. But it doesn't give the same flavour as the homemade version.

WORKING TIME: 30 minutes cooking time (this presupposes that you have some Brown Sauce and Aspic Jelly).

250 ml/8 fl oz Aspic Jelly (see page 140)
1 teaspoon gelatine
1 tablespoon sherry
300 ml/½ pt Brown Sauce (see page 134)
Salt and freshly ground black pepper

Heat up the Aspic Jelly and melt the gelatine. Add the sherry to it. Stir this mixture into the Brown Sauce and let it simmer for about 5 minutes. Strain it through a sieve and add a little salt and pepper to taste.

Brown or White Gravy

MAKES ABOUT 1.4 LITRES/2½ PT

NOT everybody likes gravy; the Reverend Sydney Smith obviously had an aversion to it. 'Madam, I have been looking for somebody who dislikes gravy all my life; let us swear eternal friendship.'

WORKING TIME: 15 minutes preparation time. 3 hours cooking time.

FOR BROWN GRAVY
4 or 5 bones (beef, lamb and/or knuckle of veal)
100 g/4 oz bacon pieces

FOR WHITE GRAVY
4 or 5 chicken bones
white breast and dark meat of chicken

2 carrots
1 large onion
2 cloves
Salt and freshly ground black pepper
Sprinkle of mace
¼ teaspoon chopped thyme
¼ teaspoon chopped sage
1 tablespoon flour

Put the bones into a heavy saucepan. Add the bacon pieces (or the white and dark chicken meat for a white gravy). Slice the carrot and the onion and put them in the saucepan with the herbs, pepper and spices.

If you are making brown gravy cover the saucepan and set it over a moderate heat for about 10 minutes to brown the bones. You have to shake the pan most of the time. Don't brown the bones for white gravy.

Sprinkle the tablespoon of flour on to the bones through a sieve and pour in enough water to cover the bones.

Put the lid on the saucepan and simmer gently for 3 hours. Strain the gravy through a cloth. Take off any fat.

Sauce Hollandaise

MAKES ABOUT 300 ML/½ PT

WORKING TIME: About 8 minutes cooking time.

2 egg yolks
100 g/4 oz butter
2 teaspoons lemon juice

Heat some water in a saucepan and stand a bowl in it. Don't let the water boil.

Put the egg yolks in the bowl and beat them with a wire whisk. Add the butter little by little, beating all the time.

Heat is the most important part of making a Hollandaise. As the sauce becomes hot and thick remove from the heat. Continue beating all the time. If the sauce is slow to thicken increase the heat. When you have added all the butter, add the lemon juice.

Bread Sauce

MAKES 300 ML/½ PT

WORKING TIME: 1 hour cooking time.

1 onion
4 cloves
600 ml/1 pt milk
100 g/4 oz white breadcrumbs
2 tablespoons butter
Salt and freshly ground black pepper
1 tablespoon double cream

Peel the onion and stick the cloves into it. Put it in a saucepan and pour the milk over. Bring slowly to the boil. Add the breadcrumbs.

Let the pan stand on the coolest ring, off the heat really, for about an hour, or until the sauce thickens. Remove the onion and add the butter and seasoning over low heat. Stir the sauce as you add the cream to bring it to a nice consistency.

Aspic Jelly

MAKES ABOUT 900 ML/1½ PT

I'M really quite ashamed to tell how I strain my aspic. I'm sure there are many wonderful new inventions on which you can tie your muslin cloth but I have never looked for them because an upturned kitchen stool has worked very well for many years.

WORKING TIME: 30 minutes preparation and cooking time.

1 onion
1 carrot
1 stalk celery
Rind and juice of 1 lemon
900 ml/1½ pt Brown Stock (see page 126)
Whites and shells of 2 eggs
¼ teaspoon mace
1 bayleaf
4 cloves
12 peppercorns
1 teaspoon gelatine
150 ml/¼ pt sherry
1 tablespoon tarragon vinegar

Peel the onion and scrape the celery and the carrot. Cut up the vegetables and place in a bowl. Squeeze the lemon into the bowl and grate the peel; throw away the pith.

Melt the stock in a saucepan (it should be a jelly), but do not let it boil. Whip the whites of the eggs and crush the shells. Add, with the rest of the ingredients, to the saucepan. Stir with a wire whisk until the gelatine has melted; continue to whisk until it boils. Allow it to simmer gently for 15 minutes.

Upturn the stool, tie the four corners of the muslin to the feet and put a bowl underneath the cloth. First pour some boiling water through the cloth and throw it away, then strain the jelly. If it isn't clear the first time pass it through again.

Don't stir the jelly while it's passing through the cloth. Let it cool and set.

Homemade Yoghurt

MAKES 1.15 LITRES /2 PT

TO make homemade yoghurt, you need a good heavy pot, a yoghurt thermometer and 2 wide-necked thermos flasks.

WORKING TIME: 35 minutes preparation and cooking time. 8 hours resting time.

1.15 litres/2 pt cartons Channel Island milk
2 tablespoons live yoghurt

Bring the milk to the boil, then turn down the heat and let it simmer, stirring occasionally. Reduce it by one third. This will take 30 minutes or so. Then bring it to the boil again. Set the yoghurt to one side to cool until it reaches between 43°C/109°F and 49°C/120°F.

Put half the milk in each thermos. Add a tablespoon of live yoghurt and stir briskly. Then put the thermos flasks on one side and don't disturb them for 8 hours.

Put the thermos flasks in the fridge after the yoghurt has formed. You can add fruit to your yoghurt, if you like, and you can now use your own yoghurt for starting your next batch.

Chantilly Cream

MAKES ABOUT 450 ML/¾PT

WORKING TIME: 10 minutes preparation time.

300 ml/½ pt double cream
5 tablespoons milk
75 g/3 oz caster sugar
2 teaspoons vanilla essence
2 tablespoons grated dark chocolate

Whip the cream and the milk together until quite frothy. Add the sugar and continue to whip.

Add the vanilla essence. You should now whip the mixture until it is thick. Chill it in the fridge until you are ready to use it.

Vanilla Syrup

MAKES ABOUT 300 ML/½ PT

8 tablespoons sugar
2 teaspoons vanilla essence

Boil the sugar and 600 ml (1 pt) water together, and reduce the liquid until it becomes syrupy. If you put a metal spoon into the mixture, it should form a thread as you take it out.

Add the vanilla essence and remove from the heat.

INDEX OF RECIPE NAMES